SHIPWRECKS OF LAKE ERIE

SHIPWRECKS OF LAKE ERIE

Tragedy in the Quadrangle

DAVID FREW

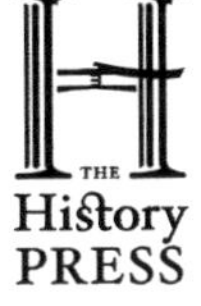

Published by The History Press
Charleston, SC 29403
www.historypress.net

Cover image courtesy of Georgann S. Wachter, www.eriewrecks.com.

First published 2014

Manufactured in the United States

ISBN 978.1.62619.551.6

Library of Congress CIP data applied for.

Notice: The information in this book is true and complete to the best of our knowledge. It is offered without guarantee on the part of the author or The History Press. The author and The History Press disclaim all liability in connection with the use of this book.

To my wife, Mary Ann Frew, my longtime academic colleague, writing partner and best friend.

CONTENTS

PREFACE
THE LAKE ERIE QUADRANGLE

Twenty years ago, a remarkable series of events altered my life. Like most university professors, I was engaged in the writing of grants, journal articles and textbooks, but as career enhancing as these projects were, there was something missing. The articles often resulted in snarky bickering by colleagues who disagreed with esoteric points, and while I had achieved success as a textbook writer, there is nothing as dull as editing and revising textbooks. As an added frustration, my choice of working at a medium-sized university, not known as a major research mill, often influenced the struggle to find grant funds.

Then, in a strange set of circumstances that connected my love of sailing and Lake Erie with academics, I fell into the company of a character from Ontario who was called the "Beachcomber of Long Point." Dave Stone, who was old enough to be my father, had carved out a niche among shipwreck enthusiasts by virtue of episodic beach deposits that appeared near his summer home on the base of Long Point, Ontario. When something interesting washed up, he dedicated countless hours to trying to determine where it came from. During an era that preceded the sophistication that currently surrounds diving and wreck hunting, his "methodology" involved waiting for Lake Erie storms and then watching as shipwreck debris washed ashore. The twenty-five-mile Long Point beachfront served as a collector for bits of shipwrecks that rose to the surface during storms, and when such debris appeared, Dave would try to identify it, date it and then determine where it had come from based on wind and wave conditions. Using this

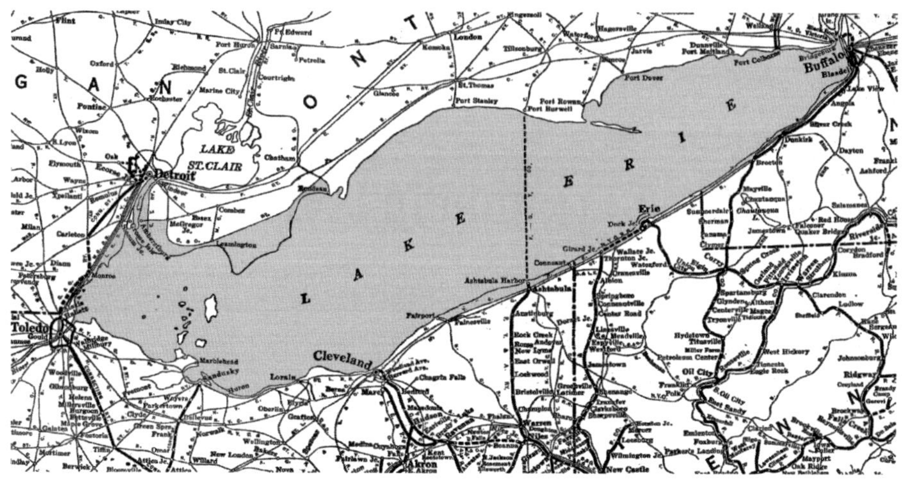

Lake Erie, the setting for shipping, shipwrecks and adventure, contained the busiest trade route in the world during the late 1800s. *Courtesy of Jerry Skrypzak.*

crude technology, he would launch one of his two boats and try to track down the underwater location of the wreck that had shed the debris.

Dave's work attracted the attention of an Ontario publishing house, which persuaded him to write a book entitled *Long Point: Last Port of Call.* While Dave was a true character—of the type made famous by the Captain Quint role that actor Robert Shaw played in the film classic *Jaws*—he was neither a writer nor a skillful organizer. And yet the book was successful by virtue of the subject matter. Dave often referred to the year that it took him to write his book as "a living hell" from which he thought he would never be released. When we met, he told me that he would never take on another writing project, but he also expressed disappointment for not properly organizing his book and for leaving some of the best stories out.

I was drawn to Dave Stone, and as our friendship grew, I began to accompany him on shipwreck-hunting adventures. But as we began to spend time hunting shipwrecks, Dave seemed to become ill. He lost fifty pounds and began to hack and cough, not entirely surprising considering that he was a chain smoker. Convinced that the illness was going to consume him, I began to talk with him about collaborating on another book. I argued that the two of us could make short work of a bigger book with a U.S. publisher and that with his stories and my writing and research skills, his wisdom could find a larger audience. As we talked about his fragile health, I struggled to convince him that as the guru of Lake Erie shipwrecks, he couldn't allow his stories to disappear. By the time he agreed, I had secured a grant to help fund the research and a regional publisher.

Our book, *The Lake Erie Quadrangle: Waters of Repose*, was released in late 1993, just in time for the holiday season, and it was a hit. Almost overnight, Dave Stone and I were celebrated as the perfect pair of authors: the old-timer with stories coupled with an academic protégé who could do research. The book was a regional bestseller, and it won national and state history awards. But the best outcome was Dave Stone's health. Apparently, the new excitement was the tonic that he needed. His health rebounded, and while he never regained the weight that he lost, his energy and enthusiasm returned.

As I wrote *Lake Erie Quadrangle*, which was well out of my academic discipline (organizational psychology), I considered the project to be a onetime departure and planned to make a quick return to my traditional work on leadership and management. But as the book moved forward, its inertia resulted in offers to do more stories on Lake Erie ships, shipping and shipwrecks. While Dave Stone steadfastly refused to become involved in other writing projects and contented himself with touring to talk about our Quadrangle adventures, I semi-reluctantly began to work on more shipwreck adventures. A series of five books called the "Quadrangle Series" followed, as did four large-format pictorial books.

In 2008, I found my way to Hannah Cassilly and The History Press, where I developed my most historically oriented work to date, *Perry's Lake Erie Fleet*, a narrative dealing with the War of 1812 fleet that was stationed in Erie. The emphasis was on the largely untold events that happened after the 1813 Battle of Lake Erie. In speaking to Hannah at The History Press after that book was completed, she suggested that I write a new book about Lake Erie shipwrecks, and I mulled over the prospect. I had no interest in reworking old stories, but there was a bothersome aspect of the Quadrangle project. In working with an established database, as I had been advised to do by academic historians, I had inadvertently "missed" several important details. While the Lloyd's of London actuarial database that we used to list the wrecks helped to anchor the previously disjointed work of Dave Stone in an objective system of qualitative research that could be defended on an academic basis, the data that we used did not include commercial fishing, yachting, excursion boats or other unreported tragedies.

The more I considered the opportunity to revisit the Lake Erie Quadrangle and take the opportunity to update the research and stories that Dave Stone and I told twenty years ago, the more exciting the project began to seem. And so, I offer a fresh look at the shipwrecks of Lake Erie and new twists on old stories, as well as a tribute to my friend, the "Beachcomber of Long Point," who passed away a few years ago.

ACKNOWLEDGEMENTS

Books don't just happen. It takes lots of help from friends and colleagues to put them together. This project would not have been possible without the help of the following special contributors.

Jerry Skrypzak made the illustrations work. His collaboration has been essential in my recent projects. I also owe a debt to Mercyhurst University, my academic home, and in particular to my colleagues Gil Jacobs, Anne Zaphiris, Missy Breckenridge and Jessica Horan-Kunko. As usual, my wife and sometime coauthor, Mary Ann Frew, read drafts and made final editions better. Thanks are owed to my friends at the Port Dover Harbour Museum for their help, in particular Ian Bell, Angela Wallace and Kerri Wamsley. Michael and Georgann Wachter and Eric Guerrin helped with shipwreck stories and images, and Melinda Meyer, Bill Nadrofsky and David Wallace also contributed. Finally, to my children and grandchildren, who have shared my sailing life, I offer these stories to enrich their lives and anchor them to their geographic roots, especially the grandkids: Abigail, Adrian, Colin, Eden, Elle, Hudson, Jordi, Noah and Phineaus. Someday, when they read them to their own children, I will have done the important job of passing Lake Erie stories along.

PART I
LAKE ERIE SHIPWRECKS

Meeting the Beachcomber: The Shipwreck Capital of the World

I grew up on Erie, Pennsylvania's industrial waterfront. For me, the waterfront and its docks represented a land of adventure, and the ships that passed through the harbor were magical. As the 1950s melded into the 1960s, the typical ships, fish tugs, sand dredges and tugboats were joined by oceangoing ships—"saltys," as locals referred to them. The opening of the St. Lawrence Seaway connected the Great Lakes to the world's oceans, and suddenly the romance of my hometown docks was enhanced by ships carrying flags of distant nations. While several of my friends gravitated toward careers on the Great Lakes as merchant sailors, I had other ideas. I decided on college and enrolled locally, where I became an engineer. Meanwhile, I met my wife, Mary Ann, and as we wandered the docks together and visited Presque Isle State Park, she became infected with my love of Lake Erie.

In 1968, I reluctantly left Erie for graduate school in Ohio, a doctoral degree and a new career. At the time, I was concerned that I would be bidding Lake Erie goodbye forever, but with three small children, I was more concerned about finding a career in which I would be available for my family; university teaching held that promise. In 1970, as I was

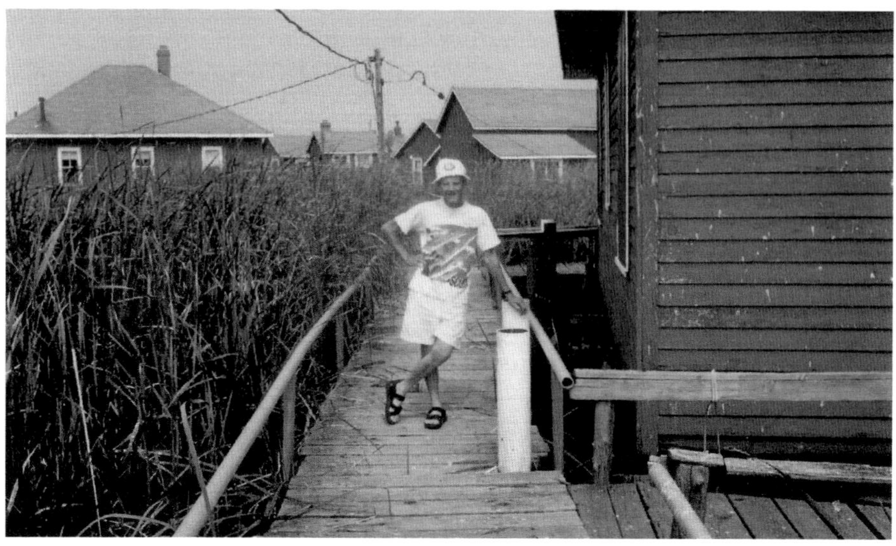

Dave Stone at the Long Point Company. *Photograph by David Frew.*

completing my doctorate, there was an opportunity to return to Erie and my alma mater, Gannon University, which was in the process of developing a graduate MBA program. Mary Ann and I jumped at the chance to return to Lake Erie, where we imagined that we could create a lovely lifestyle for our children—one in which we would expose them to the delights of life on the shores of a Great Lake.

Upon arrival, one of our first acquisitions was a sailboat. It was a bit of a splurge, but we reasoned that we would be able to use it as a tool to expose our children to the beauties and mysteries of life on the water. Our first boat, which gave way to larger and more trip-worthy vessels, was large enough for our family to sleep aboard, and as we developed our sailing skills, we ventured farther from home. Since Lake Erie's prevailing winds are from the southwest, along the axis of the lake, the easiest sailboat trips from Erie are north toward the Canadian side of the lake, so as we began to make week- and month-long boating odysseys, we gravitated toward the Long Point area and its sheltered ports. Port Dover and Port Rowan were our favorites, and we often spent several days at each on summer adventures.

In 1980, while we were at Port Rowan's municipal docks, my son returned to the boat after a shopping trip with an "amazing find." The downtown hardware store was displaying a chart of Lake Erie shipwrecks detailing names, dates and locations. After unfurling his new possession on the table inside our boat, we mulled over the chart, noticing how many of the wrecks were close to Long Point. Later, we walked to the store where my son had purchased the chart and learned that the creator of the shipwreck map was a local named Dave Stone. We also learned that Mr. Stone—"the Beachcomber," as he was known—was giving an evening lecture at the provincial park a few days later. We bummed a ride and found ourselves in front-row seats as Dave Stone gave his talk, an event that altered my life. Dave was a master storyteller. As he projected the slides, which illustrated stories of Lake Erie's most exciting shipwrecks, the crowd was spellbound. On the way home, I decided that I had just witnessed one of the greatest storytellers in the world, a skill that I needed for my own teaching career.

Back at the university, I found myself wondering how I could bring Dave Stone to Erie, and as luck would have it, I was appointed chairman of the Graduate School Speaker Series, with a generous budget reserved for speakers. That winter, I asked Dave to visit Erie and give a talk, and as optimistic as I was about the topic, I could not have anticipated the response. We booked him into a room that held five hundred people, a venue where we were usually pleased to attract crowds of one hundred. On the evening of Dave's talk, however, we filled the room and then allowed people to sit in the aisles and stand in the back. Even with that, we were forced to turn people away. Dave did not disappoint. After two hours of beachcomber stories, people remained glued to their seats for questions and answers.

That time in Erie was the beginning of a long friendship between Dave and me, and the next spring, I began an extended series of visits with him. I would drive to Long Point several times per year, meet Dave and accompany him on beachcombing adventures. We hunted for shipwrecks, wandered the beaches and hiked the interior of Long Point. During the next decade, we also traveled together to shipwreck expos, visited museums and conspired on a Canadian Grant. In 1989, with the assistance of Dave Stone and his connections, I was able to win a grant from the Canadian government that was designed to bring Canada and its business culture to the attention of American graduate students. Naturally, my approach to the month-long immersion program was to take graduate students to the Long Point area for an international experience, and we met locals and learned from them. Of course, one of the program's star Canadian professors was Dave Stone.

On one of my first wreck-hunting visits to Dave Stone's Long Point cottage, we stopped at his rural mailbox en route to the boathouse. The plan that day was to make a long run in his boat, the *Beachcomber*, to the tip of Long Point, where we were going to dive on the *Elpheke* and two other shallow-water wrecks near Gravelly Bay. The bundle of mail that Dave extracted from his box included a new shipwreck book written by a Michigan man, and as I drove, Dave began to turn the pages.

"This guy just doesn't get it," Dave muttered as I drove. "Look at this. He thinks that the most wrecks are right here on Lake Michigan," he continued, holding up a map that was attached to the new book.

"What do you think?" I asked, as Dave rustled through more pages.

"No doubt about it," Dave answered, "Lake Erie is the shipwreck capital of the world, and the very most dangerous place is right here between Long Point and Erie!"

The protégé in me wanted to believe Dave Stone, guru of shipwrecks, but when I returned to my office a few days later with a resolve to buy my own copy of the book, the skeptical academic in me decided to do some research. The research went badly. After countless hours in the 1990 world of academic history, I learned that shipwrecks were the stuff of adventurers and novelists, not traditional researchers. The closest I could come to finding peer-reviewed academic research was in a few esoteric journals of economics. Shipwrecks were financial disasters and, as such, were sometimes connected to the companies and sectors that suffered because of them. By the same token, there was nothing in the 1990 literature that could dispute Dave Stone's hypothesis that Lake Erie, and in particular a central portion of the lake (away from the western and eastern ends, where ships could turn back when faced with deteriorating weather), was the epicenter.

Since those primitive days, much has changed in the world of Great Lakes ships, shipping and shipwrecks. Recent research suggests that there are between 6,000 and 25,000 Great Lakes shipwrecks. This enormous range suggests some of the difficulty in the research. There are few such discrepancies that would feature a range (19,000) three times as large as the low estimate (6,000). In focusing just on Lake Erie, a similar range emerges. The Great Lakes Historical Museum estimates the number of Lake Erie shipwrecks at between 1,400 and 8,000. Again the range of 6,600 exceeds the low estimate by more than a factor of four. The reasons for the huge discrepancies are correlated with the root causes of the shipwrecks. Most of the disasters occurred long before modern actuarial reporting and were often underreported or misreported.

Several modern websites have been developed by shipwreck enthusiasts. One of the best, compiled by David Swayze, itemizes disasters by Great Lake. Swayze's data suggest that Lake Erie, at 23 percent of total documented wrecks, is second to Lake Michigan at 24 percent and tied with Lake Huron at 23 percent. The Swayze website is illustrative of changes that have evolved in the digital world since my 1990 research. These days, almost anyone can instantly access almost anything, including shipwrecks, via the Internet.

In examining Swayze's data, however, one possible systematic omission from his list (like our original in 1990) is the large number of commercial fish tugs that sunk in Lake Erie but were not officially reported. Of all the Great Lakes, Lake Erie was the most important center of commercial fishing and the place where fish tug technology evolved during the late 1800s and early 1900s. Another Lake Erie issue that might have contributed to underreporting of disasters was the fact that Lake Erie was the shallowest and least remote Great Lake. This led to circumstances where ships that wrecked in shallow water were often salvaged and placed back in service.

To the Dave Stone supposition that Lake Erie was the epicenter of wrecks, the absolute answer is still not clear. But if Lake Erie is not the shipwreck capital of the world, it is close to it. And regardless of the status of the overall lake as the epicenter of wrecks, it may still be that the Lake Erie Quadrangle represents the disaster bull's-eye. Swayze also did an analysis of official recorded reasons for shipwrecks, but his work was technical, including such contributory causes as storms, explosions, fire, collisions and ice; he did not deal with the macro factors that might help explain the unique treachery of Lake Erie. The geography of the lake, in which its longitudinal axis is exactly the same as the southwesterly to northeasterly current, quickly churns its shallow waters into a frenzy, especially in a nor'easter.

Inventing the Quadrangle: Adding a Database to Lake Erie's Shipwreck Research

My Canadian studies grant required academic output (publications), and given my evolving relationship with Dave Stone, I began to chat with him about a new book. His *Long Point: Last Port of Call* project had been less than fun for him, and he was reluctant, but calling attention to untold stories that had not made it into his first book, I eventually talked him into a collaboration in which I would do the writing. My personal struggle was justifying the effort professionally. I would be wandering well outside my organizational psychology and leadership boundaries, but the opportunity to do something so exciting and connected to my love of Lake Erie was irresistible.

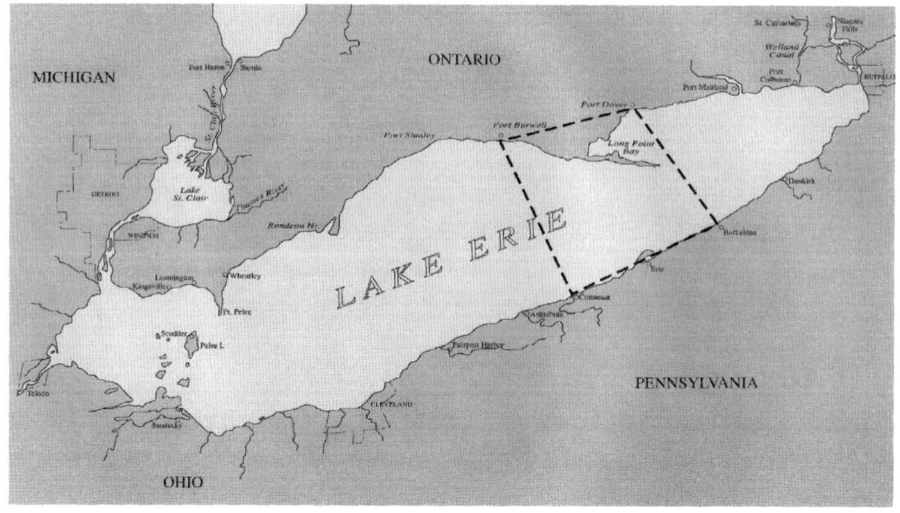

The Lake Erie Quadrangle, outlined here on a map of Lake Erie, originally contained 429 registered Lloyd's of London shipwrecks in only 2,500 square miles. *Courtesy of Jerry Skrypzak.*

For advice, I went to my boss, Academic Vice President Dr. Robert Wall. Robert, who was a Canadian citizen, was both a friend and an accomplished historian. He had already encouraged me to connect my love of Canada with my academic life, and he inspired me by commenting that since much of my previous writing seemed more like engineering reports than readable narratives, a shipwreck project might be exactly what I needed. He went on to say that in his final teaching position before ascending to the world of academic administration, his favorite class was research methods in history.

I was dumbstruck. History and research methods? I had never connected the two.

"You're stuck in a mindset that the only research is quantitative," Wall explained. "You need a tutorial in qualitative methods."

Robert loaned me a qualitative methods book. I took it home to study, and the next few weeks of his tutelage altered my academic life forever. I began to uncover the mysteries of qualitative research and the power of narrative storytelling for uncovering theory. I was already trying to be more of a storyteller during lectures, largely because of my time with Dave Stone, so the material fell on eager ears. As I continued, Robert offered an important admonition: "Don't move forward without a database that can be replicated."

When I asked about finding such a tool, he added a clue, one that I had already considered. "Follow the money, and you will usually uncover the realities of history."

"Of course," I thought to myself, "I was teaching MBA students. Where else would I find reliable data? Every shipwreck was an economic event!"

After a brief search, the best source became obvious: Lloyd's of London. In the emerging world of nineteenth-century shipping, Lloyd's was a central resource for merchant sailors and shipowners. Originally located in London, the epicenter of European commerce, Lloyd's served as an information clearinghouse, insurance agency and actuarial arm for the world's shipping economy. It even offered an early version of shipping news, a periodical aimed at shippers and merchants. When shipping exploded on the Great Lakes, and the trade route between Buffalo and Detroit became the busiest in the world during the mid-1800s, Lloyd's opened a branch in Cleveland, Ohio, so that it would be closer to the action.

Armed with the Lloyd's early 1900s summary of Lake Erie wrecks, which included general descriptions of disaster locations, I solicited the assistance of university computer wizards, who located each wreck on a wall-sized computer screen. To the official Lloyd's list, we added the few dozen wrecks that we were aware of thanks to Dave Stone's previous research. Even then, however, we recognized two problems. Lloyd's ceased to be the primary insurer of North American shipping during the mid-1800s, and by the early 1900s, it was no longer engaged in recording all Great Lakes disasters, regardless of insurance carrier. The second weakness was connected to the Lloyd's locations, which were crude at best. News accounts would often place the actual locations miles away from the Lloyd's approximations, but we consistently used the official records, partially because of the unreliability of the old newspapers.

Even with the possible flaws in our computer-based system, however, we had a screen full of Lake Erie shipwrecks, and we were ready for the next step. Smitten by popular stories of the Bermuda Triangle, we decided to try to identify a similar place in Lake Erie—a relatively small geographic area that would stand out because of the density of shipwrecks. The traditional mathematical approach to such a problem involved calculus, so I shanghaied a team of math professors and began to manipulate the field of Lake Erie shipwrecks on the computer screen in a search for Lake Erie's version of the Bermuda Triangle.

Within a few minutes, we had it. There, in the center of the lake between Erie and Long Point, was a pulsating green computer screen segment that said it all. According to the mathematics and the Lloyd's data, a nondescript portion of the lake bounded by Ashtabula, Ohio, and Dunkirk, New York, on the north shore and by Port Stanley and Dunnville, Ontario, on the Canadian shore contained the highest density of shipwrecks in the smallest relative area of Lake Erie.

Our discovery wasn't a triangle. The uneven angles of boundary lines projected across the lake from the area's western and eastern extremities did not reveal a square or even a traditional rectangle. But it was a bounded shape that we could justify with replicable data. But what to call it? Rushing across campus from the computer lab to my office to phone Dave Stone and tell him the news, I found myself passing through an area that is common to many university campuses: the Quadrangle or "Quad," as students called it. It was an amorphous gathering place between campus buildings and a common area for between-class chitchat, parties and gatherings. "Why not?" I thought to myself. We would name our discovery the "Lake Erie Quadrangle."

We had "discovered" a 2,500-square-mile segment of Lake Erie with 429 official Lloyd's of London shipwrecks. The Lake Erie Quadrangle made the Bermuda Triangle seem wimpy.

Between the Cracks: Some Things that We Missed

The Quadrangle book project went smoothly. Dave Stone's stories flowed, the database helped us devise a comprehensive list and our publisher pushed to make the book happen for the 1993 holiday season. To our amazement, the book was a success on both sides of the lake. Interestingly, the success proved to be a double-edged sword. As sales increased and both Dave Stone and I began to receive unsolicited offers to do promotional talks and book signings, a less positive downside began to emerge in the form of corrections. Some of the corrections that we received were linked to the imprecision of the Lloyd's locations. We had located the *Oneida*, for example, in thirty feet of water well off the beaches of Freeport, Pennsylvania. Shortly after the book was released, a local sent a picture of himself standing on *Oneida*'s boiler, less than one hundred yards from shore, with only his lower legs showing. "Dear experts," his letter began, "in case you want to know where the *Oneida* really is, give me a call."

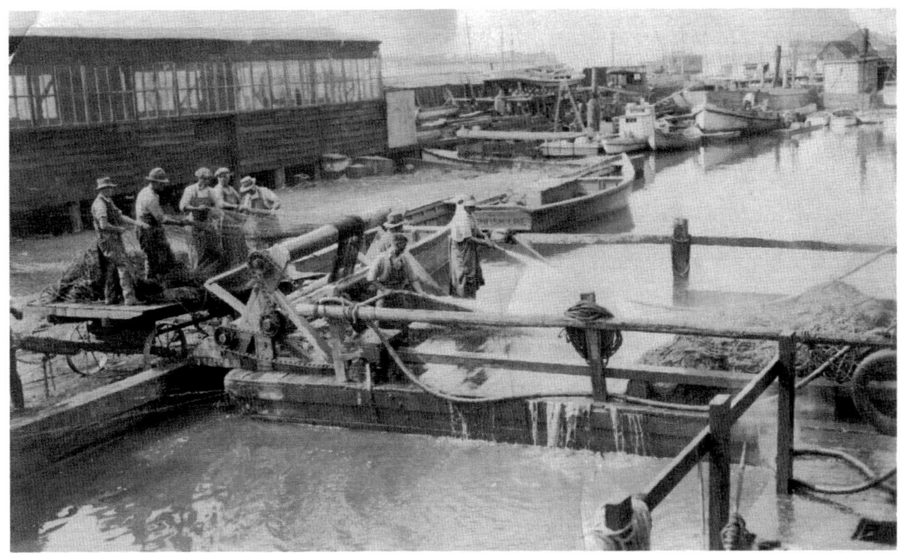

Commercial fishing accidents from ports such as Erie, as it looked here in 1910, accounted for most of the shipwrecks that we missed. *Courtesy of Jerry Skrypzak.*

In further investigating the loss of the *Oneida* in old newspapers, we learned that the owner-captain, Thomas Black, was suspected of igniting his own ship for the insurance. Apparently, he had temporarily anchored *Oneida* close to the beaches, where he could easily make it to the safety of shore and then hope for the wind to carry the burning hull offshore. While the ship actually sank close to shore, his report to Lloyd's made it look like he had been forced to abandon ship offshore using the lifeboats. In another example, the Wachters, now famous Lake Erie wreck hunters, sent an underwater photo of the *James Colgate* showing it to be fifty miles from where we had indicated.

Our response that we had used an official database failed to satisfy those who argued that replicable data was not as important as providing precise locations for divers. Little did we know that in a decade, modern websites would list easily accessed locations, and the Wachters would become prolific authors of books on underwater Lake Erie wreck sites. Since our 1990 work, websites dedicated to Lake Erie shipwrecks have operated like modern wikis (Wikipedia, for example), where participants are encouraged to enhance and adjust the information that is presented. Shipwreck locations have also benefited from enhancements in location technology, first with LORAN (**LO**ng **RA**nge **N**avigation) and now with extremely accurate GPS headings.

The objections related to our use of the database were not as bothersome, however, as calls and letters informing us of things that we missed. Some of the omissions were glaring and had taken place almost under our noses. The losses of the fish tugs *Mary Lou* in Erie and *Grace M* near Long Point were examples. The explanation for our "omissions" was related to the limitations of the Lloyd's inclusions. During the 1800s, Lloyd's insisted on including every Great Lakes disaster regardless of insurance carrier so that it could calculate the risks and insurance fees for ships and cargos. It did not, however, continue this practice after World War I, nor did it include fish tugs, work boats and private yachts. We had made an attempt to add as many of those as we could when we did the 1990 research, but United States and Canadian Coast Guard records were sketchy at best, and the commercial fishing associations were not well organized enough to provide reliable data.

In defense of Dave Stone's original assertion that the middle of Lake Erie was the epicenter of shipwrecks, the additions that were streaming into our revised database provided even more support. Within months, we had an additional 45 shipwrecks to add to the original list of 459, and many of the additions were fish tugs. Lake Erie was the Great Lakes commercial fishing hot spot, and the ports within the Lake Erie Quadrangle—including Ashtabula, Barcelona, Conneaut, Dunkirk, Erie, Port Burwell, Port Dover and Port Stanley—were among the busiest fishing centers on the lake. Of course there should have been a number of fish tugs in our wreck list! For several decades during the early 1900s, Erie was the "freshwater fishing capital of the world."

Evolutions in Dive Technology: The Rare Intact Wreck Sites

I am not a diver. On several occasions, after being strapped by well-intentioned friends into SCUBA gear, I have descended to the awesome depths of a standard swimming pool or drifted down onto shallow wrecks to experience the "freedom" of diving with the support of oxygen. I am a good swimmer and comfortable with the regulated breathing of a mouthpiece, but given the choice of a free-dive to see fish on a Caribbean reef versus lowering myself into murky, gray water to look at a shipwreck, I would choose snorkeling every time. The thought of descending one hundred or

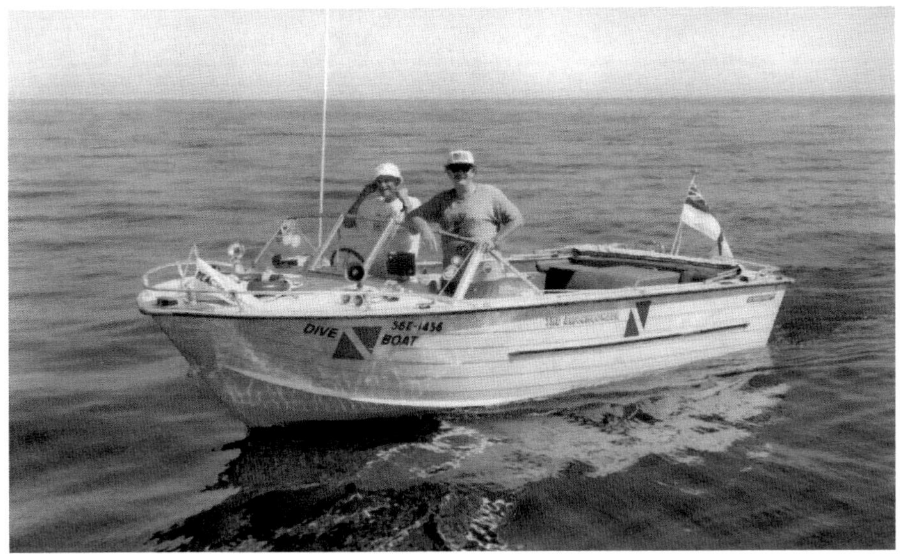

Dave Stone and me in *Beachcomber*, off on a wreck-hunting expedition. *Photograph by John Mitchell.*

more feet into the depths of Lake Erie and passing beyond the technical one-atmosphere limits, where decompression dangers lurk, is beyond frightening to me. I admire the bravery, dedication and skill of divers like Mike Fletcher, Gary Kosak and the Wachters (Mike and Georgann), who have plumbed the depths of Lake Erie in the search for shipwrecks and their stories, but my job will continue to be storytelling.

Like Dave Stone, I grew up watching television episodes of *Seahunt* and later became excited by the notion that Lake Erie could contain the same kinds of shipwrecks that spawned those 1950s adventures. Unlike the oceans or *Seahunt* episodes, however, there was no visibility. Mike Fletcher once told me that when he first began to explore the 165-foot wreck of the steamer *Atlantic*, he was barely able to see the fingers of his hand with the powerful light that he carried.

When Dave Stone and I began our Quadrangle research in 1990, the divers we contacted were less than forthcoming. When we asked about particular wrecks, there was a culture of secrecy. The reluctance may have been created by the extreme difficulty encountered in finding the rare deep-water wreck sites. To learn about individual wrecks, we often had to "ask a guy who knew another guy, who might meet us in a bar." Even when we found our way to the right diver, the descriptions were vague if not disguised.

Of all the people we met, Mike Fletcher, who had spent years hunting for the steamer *Atlantic*, was the most forthcoming. He had known Dave Stone for years and was somehow not threatened by the college professor who was tagging along. After all the time that Mike had invested in hunting for the shipwreck of his childhood dreams, he had the most to protect, but Mike was generous with his descriptions of the *Atlantic* and other Lake Erie shipwrecks. And of all the people we met, he was the most thorough researcher.

Mike's underwater footage of the *Atlantic* revealed a dark and dangerous world. His access to the wreck and ability to spend time on it was enabled by his professional diving skills, equipment and experience. Unlike most of the divers we were meeting at the time, Mike Fletcher was a hard-hat diver with backup safety systems, a sophisticated dive boat and a recompression chamber. This was what allowed him to make deep dives and spend as much time as he did on each descent. His target ship, the steamer *Atlantic*, while an amazing treasure with stories to tell, bore little resemblance to the ship-in-a-bottle vision that I had always imagined. The *Atlantic*, while protected by its location in deep water, was beat up and damaged from the original sinking, as well as by the crude and thoughtless attempts by early salvers, including a crew of men in one-atmosphere suits. Even after Mike had begun diving the *Atlantic*, less than thoughtful divers followed him to the deck in SCUBA gear, used the few minutes that they had at the extreme depth to attach grappling hooks and lines to deck features and then attempted to retrieve souvenirs by ripping at them from the surface. Much of the modern damage done to the *Atlantic* was thoughtless and sad.

Even as Mike Fletcher was working on the *Atlantic* during the 1980s, changes altered the environment near the ship. Zebra and other mussels began to proliferate at the wreck site and clarify the water. Soon, the visibility had improved to the point that divers could descend to the wreck and begin to see the outlines of the ship from depths of only fifty or sixty feet. At the same time that this was happening during the 1990s, efforts to reverse the eutrophication of Lake Erie began to bear fruit and the entire water column began to clarify.

Other technologies emerged during the 1990s. The most important of these was the Global Positioning System (GPS), which was infinitely more accurate than the old LORAN methods of locating wrecks. Throughout the 1990s and 2000s, divers also began to share specific GPS locations and publish them on websites. Closely guarded, secret locations of shipwrecks suddenly became public knowledge, and dive charter companies began taking recreational divers to wreck sites on a regular basis. Diving equipment also improved, as more businesses offered dive training. With increased awareness of dive sites and more wrecks being located, recreational wreck diving charters soon became viable new businesses.

Of the thousands of estimated Lake Erie shipwrecks, however, very few exist in an attractive and recognizable form. Most of Lake Erie's shipwrecks took place in the shallows, where the carcasses were subsequently either raised and put back into service or left to be battered or plundered. Close-to-shore wrecks were further damaged by winter ice. It was only the deep-water and inaccessible wrecks that stood a chance of being preserved if divers could find them. How many of these wrecks are left to visit? The short answer is that no one knows. Perhaps 150 or fewer, and of those, only a few continue to resemble the ships that originally sank. Many of the most popular dive sites have been reduced to barely recognizable fragments, but they are still interesting and fun to visit. And thanks to improved clarity, recreation divers who should not risk descents of 100 or more feet can hover over the wrecks, see them and photograph them. The *Atlantic*, for example, which at 165 feet lies well beyond the prudent limits of recreational divers, can now be seen and photographed from only 50 feet below the surface.

PART II
WARTIME ON LAKE ERIE

THE SCHOONER *AMELIA* (1813): LAKE ERIE'S FIRST SHIPWRECK

Anxious to participate in the anticipated shipping economy of the Great Lakes, the State of Pennsylvania purchased a northern land extension in 1795 with almost fifty miles of Lake Erie frontage. Then it encouraged settlers to move to the new frontier town of Erie. By 1812, maritime commerce was underway, and Erie's shipping economy was thriving. The Reed family in downtown Erie had recruited Daniel Dobbins by offering him a master's share in his own schooner, the *Salina*, and he was regularly trading salt and other bulk commodities for furs and whitefish in the Georgian Bay.

As the second decade of the new century unfolded on Lake Erie, the bane of American merchant sailors was the British navy. Annoyed by the War of Independence, which had squeezed them out of the lower portion of the Americas, the British were strengthening their hold on Upper Canada (Ontario) and exercising power over the Great Lakes with an armed naval fleet. During a time before railroads and developed roadways, when most commerce was delivered by water, sailing ships provided the best method of delivery to the Northwest Territories. But the British—who knew that as a result of treaty agreements the international boundary on the Great Lakes

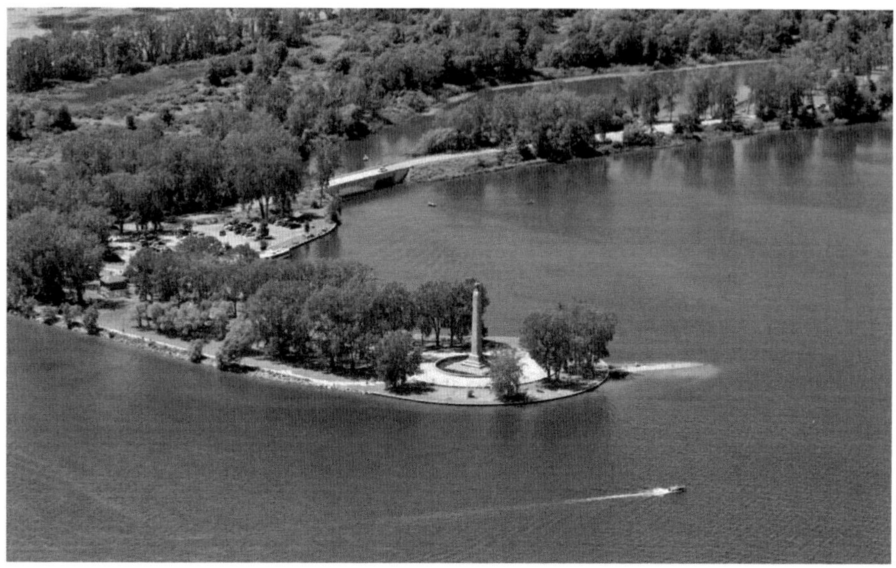

Little Bay—or Misery Bay, as it is known now—is Erie's shipwreck central. *Photograph by John Baker.*

bisected each of the upper lakes (with the exception of Lake Michigan)—decided that American ships that wandered into their territorial waters were to be arrested and detained. For masters of commercial schooners like Dobbins, who were forced to tack upwind and downwind in relatively inefficient sailing ships, it was almost impossible to avoid passing over the line, especially near the western end of Lake Erie or in the rivers leading to Lake Huron and the Georgian Bay. Dobbins, like other merchant sailors, was detained several times for such incursions; he finally had his ship seized and was taken prisoner.

Through a series of clever political manipulations, Dobbins escaped, returned to Erie and worked with his mentor and shipping company owner, Rufus Reed, to convince the United States government that an American naval fleet was needed to protect Lake Erie from the British, as well as that it should be built and housed in Erie. Instantly, a new naval base and two shipyards were created, and Erie became an integral part of the War of 1812. At the time, the population of Erie was about four hundred, while Buffalo to the east had five hundred and Cleveland to the west had fewer than two hundred.

Dobbins, who was commissioned to build the fleet, began by laying out and framing two small gunboats inside the protection of Presque Isle Bay. As he worked, he waited for a fleet commander to show up. By March, Oliver Hazard Perry had arrived with a New England shipbuilder. Seeing the progress on the new "Lake Erie fleet," Perry ordered the construction of four more ships, but even with the emerging fleet, he knew that the British, with their established Lake Erie fleet, would have the advantage. One hundred miles to the east at Buffalo (Black Rock), the United States had established a fort to support land actions along the Niagara River. The commanders there had managed to create a small naval fleet by using converted merchant ships and captured British vessels. Their fleet of five ragtag vessels included two significant ships, the seventy-five-ton *Ohio* and eighty-five-ton *Caledonia*, as well as three smaller boats: *Amelia*, *Somers* and *Trippe*. After considering his options, Perry decided that the best tactic would be to bring the Black Rock fleet to Erie to join the ships that were under construction.

The problem with fetching the five ships was that Black Rock was almost ten miles down current on the fast-moving Niagara River. To move the ships upriver into Lake Erie would be more than a daunting task, and with armed British warships patrolling the lake, Perry realized that if the enemy received word that he was engaged in the slow task of towing ships upstream to Lake Erie, they would lie in wait in the open lake and destroy them. Perry also realized that there was a British fort just across the mouth of the Niagara River from which he would be spotted if he were to take too long dispatching the ships once they were in the open lake.

In one of the most decisive judgments leading to the Battle of Lake Erie, Perry crafted a clever plan. He knew that the British fleet was prowling about near Erie, watching for signs of progress in the building of the fleet, so he departed under the cover of nightfall, marched to Buffalo (Black Rock) with a force of sailors and sent a scout, who instructed the sailors to gather in waiting and hire as many locals as could be found to help with a "secret" task. Timing their maneuver carefully, Perry and two hundred men slowly began to hopscotch the five ships up the river using tiller-men aboard the ships to steer and ropes attached to shore. His primary focus was on the *Ohio* and *Caledonia* since they were the largest and most important, but compared to the difficulty of towing those ships upstream, the smaller vessels were relatively easy, so he and his men brought them along.

Timing his entry into the open lake carefully, Perry tried to complete the last stage of his maneuver during the cover of darkness, hoping that he would not be spotted from Fort Erie. The final mile of the upriver tow took longer than had been expected, however, and he was observed. As he and his men watched, there was a visible reaction from Fort Erie. The British were too far away to launch cannon fire, but Perry knew that his lead time would be short and that horseback scouts would be rushing west to contact British naval commander Robert Heriot Barclay. As soon as the British commander received word of his activity, the British squadron would be hunting for him.

Perry assumed that he would be able to outrun and/or outmaneuver the British with his two larger ships, but he was concerned that the British commander would cull the smaller ships—the *Amelia*, *Somers* and *Trippe*—away from the American delivery fleet and destroy them. He was also concerned that if the British were on guard at Erie's channel entrance, he would have a difficult time getting past them and into the shallow harbor.

Fate was kind to Perry, who emerged from the War of 1812 with a reputation for being both incredibly brave and lucky. The British had apparently learned that Perry left town with a large force of men and concluded that they were heading for Black Rock. At about the time that Perry was emerging from the Niagara River, the British fleet was sailing downwind toward Buffalo, taking advantage of southwesterly winds to make great speed. Given the ninety-mile distance between Erie and the eastern end of the lake, it would be a matter of only half a day before Barclay would arrive to confront Perry, whose ships were not prepared for an artillery battle.

Meanwhile, Perry made the decision to depart with *Caledonia* and *Ohio* before the three small ships were ready. He was assuming that if he encountered Barclay's fleet, he could distract them, lure the British away from the smaller ships and prevent them from blockading the Erie harbor. Less than three hours into his upwind beat toward Erie, Perry's watchmen spotted sails on the horizon. In another of his daring maneuvers, Perry waited until he was within sight of the British before he tacked north, inviting the British to try to intercept him. With Perry in command of *Caledonia* and Dobbins of the *Ohio*, the two-ship American squadron led the six-ship British fleet on a tacking duel to the western base of Long Point before dousing all lights and unfurling the yards for a broad reach back toward the Erie harbor.

Perry confused Barclay when he sailed west, making the British commander think that he might be making an aggressive move toward Amhurstburg, homeport of the British fleet. Concerned that Perry might sail up the Detroit River and use cannons to destroy the British flagship, *Detroit*, which was under construction, Barclay sailed for the western end of the lake to protect his own fort.

Meanwhile, on the eastern end of the lake, the three small American ships were slowly tacking along the American shore toward Erie. During the evening of Perry's maneuver that outfoxed Barclay, the smaller ships made steady progress. At first light, the *Somers* and *Trippe*, which had sailed within sight of each other, successfully entered the harbor. Perry and Dobbins followed shortly in *Caledonia* and *Ohio*; the only ship unaccounted for was *Amelia*, the smallest and slowest.

By midmorning, *Amelia* had not yet appeared, and Perry decided that the captain and crew of the small gunboat had encountered difficulty and given up. There was a brisk breeze that evening, and Perry had been concerned about *Amelia*'s condition when he saw it at Black Rock.

At noon, Perry's men informed him that they had spotted sails on the horizon. To the north, at a distance of ten miles, watchmen from Little Bay, where Perry had anchored the *Caledonia* and *Ohio*, counted six sets of sails. Barclay had concluded that Perry was returning to Erie, and he was sailing back. On the eastern horizon, at a distance of less than five miles, there was a single set of sails. It had to be *Amelia*. For several hours, Perry and his men stood vigil near the channel watching the sails converge. The British had the advantage since they were sailing with the wind. But *Amelia* was making progress into the wind. The closer it got to Erie, however, the more the trees on Presque Isle blocked the wind, giving the British a further sailing advantage. Providentially, it seemed that the British fleet had not spotted the American gunboat as it made its punishingly slow tacks up the coast. Finally, at 4:00 p.m., the British ships seemed to drift northward and slow down, and *Amelia* tacked into the harbor, bouncing several times on the shallows as the helmsman tried desperately to minimize the number of tacks needed to fetch the harbor. With eleven ships in Erie, six under construction (including the *Lawrence* and *Niagara*) and the five newly transported from Black Rock, Perry suddenly had the advantage.

As Perry's men worked frantically to complete the ships under construction downtown and at Cascade Creek, the five-ship Black Rock squadron waited at anchor in Little Bay, where crews worked to make them battle ready. By August, when Perry was ready to move his fleet into the open lake, however, work at Little Bay had not progressed on the *Amelia*. *Caledonia* and *Ohio* were put in first-class repair, and then *Somers* and *Trippe*, but with the inevitable confrontation with the British approaching and a shortage of sailors, Perry made the decision to focus on the other ships and ignore *Amelia*.

As the ten-ship fleet departed Erie for the western end of Lake Erie and glory, *Amelia* was scuttled in Little Bay, beginning a Lake Erie tradition in which most wrecks have been near shore. It would not be alone at Little Bay. Shortly after the war, *Amelia* was joined by *Niagara*, *Lawrence*, *Caledonia* and *Lady Charlotte*. Then, as the 1800s continued, it was accompanied by a dozen canal packets and several old wooden fish tugs. By the time Little Bay was renamed Misery Bay, it had earned the reputation for being Erie's graveyard of ships.

Salina (1813): Double Spoils of War

Daniel Dobbins was recruited by Judah Colt to come to Erie in 1795. Dobbins was a bold young man who had spent time at the docks in Philadelphia, which was a major American port in those days. Since Colt had aspirations of building a shipping business in Erie, he brought Dobbins to supervise construction of his first schooners and be senior captain of his new Lake Erie fleet. As the appointed land agent sent by Pennsylvania to develop the new lakefront land, Colt had first choice of the properties adjacent to Lake Erie.

Judah Colt purchased three plots of land east of Erie. The first two included the mouths of Four Mile (Harborcreek) and Sixteen Mile (Freeport) Creeks, where he hoped to create shipping ports. His third purchase was a plot of land at the highest elevation east of Erie, on the Appalachian Escarpment Ridge. To hedge his bets, Colt later purchased land within the town of Erie, an acquisition intended to give him access to the anticipated downtown commercial center.

While Colt's business plan seemed brilliant, it was flawed. He did not purchase waterfront land inside the shelter of Erie's natural harbor since he didn't think schooner captains would be willing to tack upwind through an unimproved channel into the shelter of Presque Isle Bay. Instead, he thought that he could attract commercial ships to the major creeks east of Erie. His plan was to unload cargos and haul them up to the top of the ridge. From his vantage point at the highest point overlooking Lake Erie (today's Colt Station), he hoped to use the headwaters of French Creek to move Lake Erie goods to Pittsburgh, where he could trade for supplies that he would sell at his trading post.

By the early 1800s, Colt could see that he had made a few miscalculations. French Creek was only navigable to his upper station trading post for a few months of the year, and while he had been building the trading post on the ridge overlooking the lake, the Reeds had taken over the Erie waterfront locations that he had ignored and had begun to improve the channel.

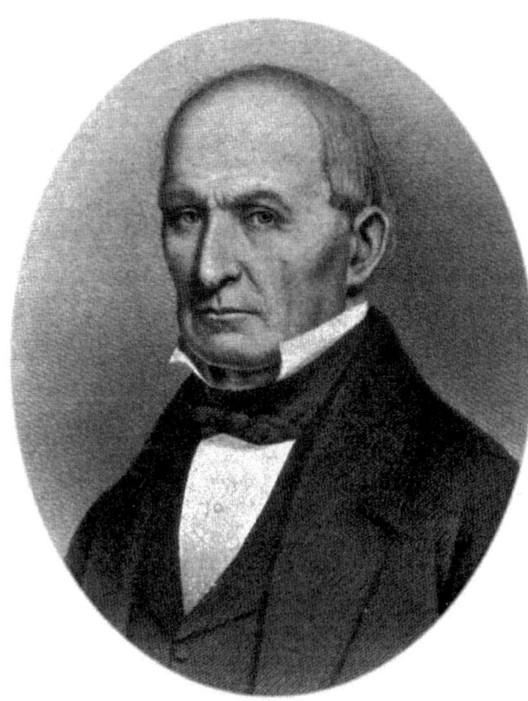

Captain Daniel Dobbins. *Courtesy of Jerry Skrypzak.*

There were also rumors of steamships that were being developed on the east end of Lake Erie—ships that would make it relatively easy to enter the shelter of Presque Isle Bay. In 1806, Colt abandoned his two lower station creek ports and changed his business to a strictly land-based trading post at the top of the ridge.

Dobbins left Colt's employ and moved to Erie, where he was welcomed by the Reeds. Rufus Reed offered him part ownership of a ship, the *Salina*, a forty-five-foot two-masted schooner. *Salina* went to work in 1809 hauling salt from Syracuse (which was delivered to Buffalo) into the Georgian Bay, where Dobbins traded for whitefish, whiskey and furs. Between 1809 and 1812, Dobbins and Reed made a fortune. One cargo of Georgian Bay furs returned to Erie in 1811, for example, was valued at $200,000. By the 1812 shipping season, Dobbins was reputed to be the most knowledgeable sailing master on the upper lakes, and since it was a tradition to reward a ship's captain with a percentage of the profit from each run, he was also a wealthy man.

In 1812, *Salina* was taken by the British on a trading run to Fort Mackinac. Unbeknownst to Dobbins, the British had taken the fort but continued to fly the American flag. When Dobbins landed, his ship was seized, and a few hours later, he and the rest of *Salina*'s crew were being ferried to Detroit without their boat or its valuable cargo. Six months later, Dobbins was in Washington, D.C., using the considerable influence of the Reed family to convince decision-makers that a Great Lakes naval fleet should be built in Erie and that he was the right man to be the architect of the fleet and building manager. At first, United States military officials were reluctant to grant permission or funding to build the new naval fleet in Erie, but

Dobbins presented a compelling case for his plan. He argued that news of the construction of a fleet of ships would quickly find its way across Lake Erie to the British and that enemy spies would be watching every move that the American builders made.

If the fleet were to be built in an established seaport—Black Rock (Buffalo), for instance—British ships would wait until construction was almost finished and then attack. In the closed seaport at Erie, because of the shallow, unimproved channel, British ships would not be able to sail within cannon range of the new fleet and blast it into splinters before it was launched. The absolute brilliance of Dobbins's plan was that Erie had just enough water in its channel to float the finished but unloaded (with cannons and supplies) ships out into the open lake but not enough depth to allow fully armed British ships to sail in. As a bonus, frontier Erie boasted massive hardwood and softwood forests growing almost to the water's edge. Thus, the lumber needed to build the ships was readily available.

Construction began during the winter of 1812, and as Dobbins had suggested, British spies made regular tours of Erie, noting progress. At first, it seemed that the task of building six naval ships from scratch in one season would be impossible, but as Dobbins and his men carried on, it became apparent that their mission might actually be accomplished since Dobbins (with Noah Brown, who came later with Perry) was on schedule to complete the fleet by August. There was one construction problem, however, and it was significant. The pine pitch (tar) needed to impregnate the running rigging took more than a year to cure, and Dobbins had not anticipated the amount that would be needed to treat the lines on all of the ships. His miscalculation was connected to changes that Perry ordered in the original plans that Dobbins had made. When Perry arrived with Noah Brown, they increased the size of the smaller ships that Dobbins had already begun and added plans to build two large ships, *Lawrence* and *Niagara*.

With spring approaching, shipwrights informed Dobbins that it would be impossible to properly treat the running rigging on *Niagara* and *Lawrence*. This was a serious problem, so disconcerting that when word of the matter reached Barclay, he joked that the American fleet would be frozen in for another winter while Dobbins cooked new tar. Dobbins would not have let that happen. If required, he would have launched the new ships with untreated running rigging, a weakness that may have caused mast and sail failures. But then everything about the construction of the American fleet was done on the rush. Green wood, design shortcuts and a host of other problems were ignored in favor of expediency. How else could a fleet be built in less than a year? Few expected the new fleet to last for more than a year or so. Its only purpose was to engage the British during the late summer of 1813.

Meanwhile, back at Amhurstburg, Dobbins's old ship, *Salina*, had been transformed by the British into a work boat used to move supplies and transport troops. Late in the spring of 1812, *Salina* was sent to Ohio to retrieve the bodies of troops who had been killed during a land battle. Winter ice was closing in as *Salina* was approaching shore near Toledo, and before the captain realized what was happening, he had sailed into pack ice and run hard aground. The crew worked for days trying to free *Salina* from the icy grip that held it less than a mile from shore; the weather worsened, though, and they finally abandoned it. By mid-January, *Salina* was frozen solid. Its hull was crushed by the force of shifting ice, the rig had fallen and the British had given up on the old salt-trader.

The winter of 1812–13 was bitter. Lake Erie was iced over by early January and frozen solid through March. But the cold temperatures did not impede construction of the fleet in Erie. Under Dobbins's and Brown's supervision, six new ships were framed and well underway by spring. If anything, the frozen ground helped the men in the shipyards as they slid heavy timbers around and worked them into place. When Lake Erie's ice floes finally began to break up and make their annual easterly pilgrimage toward the Niagara River, Dobbins's men kept watch on the water conditions along Presque Isle's shores. Their primary interest was in the water level that year, since they realized that without at least six or seven feet of draft in the channel, there would be no way to move the bigger ships (*Lawrence* and *Niagara*) out into the open lake.

In late March, Dobbins's scouts returned to the Cascade Creek shipyard with a stunning report. They had spotted an old schooner frozen in pack ice and drifted onto the beach just west of Erie. Moments after hearing this report, Dobbins was across the bay ice, onto the beaches at the base of Presque Isle and hiking west with a party of six. "Could it be?" he wondered aloud.

The moment he spotted the derelict ship, he knew that it was *Salina.* The ice floe that held his beloved schooner had broken free and sailed close to a beach amid a mass of pack ice. *Salina* was less than a half mile from shore, crushed and splintered but otherwise intact. Using anchors that were still aboard his old ship, Dobbins and his crew kedged the badly damaged schooner as close to shore as they could. Then they plodded through mushy ice to harvest its sails, rigging, metalwork and running rigging, and their fortuitous salvage contained the tar needed to complete the *Lawrence* and the *Niagara* rigging.

When they had finished removing anything that could be boiled down into new tar for the rigging, Dobbins released the anchors, gave the ice floe that held *Salina* a gentle push and sent it off with the ice to sink. Reports the next day suggested that the ice that had carried *Salina* back to its owner and delivered a gift that helped rig *Lawrence* and *Niagara* slipped below the surface of Lake Erie just east of town, where the ship's bones were destined to become one of the thousands of shipwrecks to grace the bottom of Lake Erie.

THE BRITISH PAYROLL SHIP *MOHAWK* (1814): LEGENDS OF LONG POINT GOLD

Long Point, Ontario, one of North America's most remarkable land masses, continues to be managed as a wilderness area where visitors are prohibited. During the early 1800s, the massive peninsula, which extends into the center of Lake Erie from its base near Port Rowan, Ontario, was a lawless badland. Dodgy characters used it to launch activities such as prostitution, gambling and bare-knuckle prizefights, while frontiersmen exploited the land by harvesting lumber and conducting uncontrolled market hunting of ducks, turtles, fish and mammals.

From a navigational perspective, Long Point posed a danger because of its mid-lake location. The eastward tip stretched to within a few miles of the straight-line shipping trade route between Buffalo and Detroit, and the unpredictably changing sand structure spawned shoaling hazards in two different places. The first was at the eastern tip, which was often used as a sheltering anchorage during severe storms. The shore there was largely uncharted since offshoot sandbars regularly grew out from the tip and then disappeared. The shoals were particularly hazardous to sailing schooners. The second area of danger was near the base of the peninsula, where natural cuts (channels into the protected Inner Bay) appeared and disappeared several times during the 1800s and early 1900s. The cuts provided shortcuts for tacking sailboats or steamships seeking shelter from the open waters of the lake.

As the shipping economy evolved in the 1800s, two lighthouses appeared on Long Point. One was built at the eastern tip and another near the cut(s)

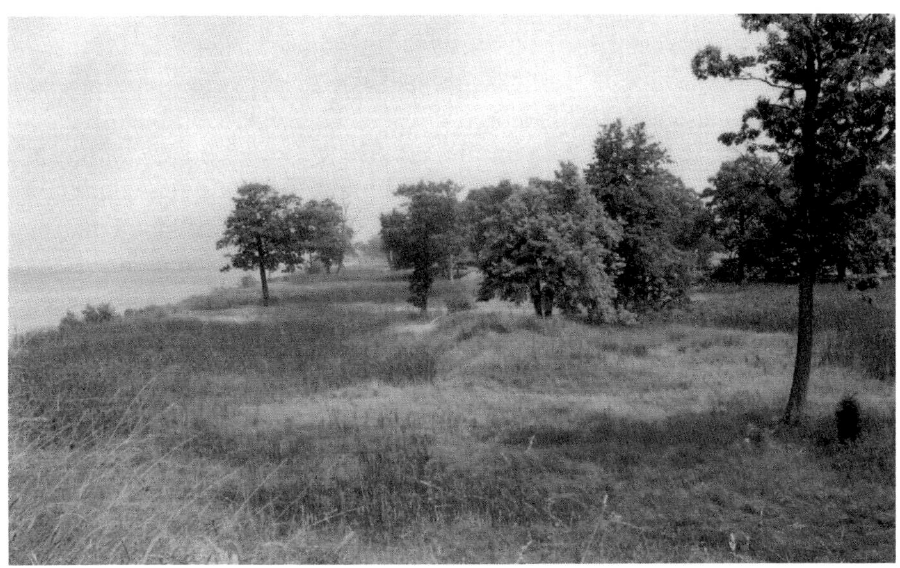

The beaches a few miles west of the tip of the point, leading to the interior of Long Point. *Photograph by David Frew.*

closer to the base. The Old Cut Lighthouse was particularly problematic for shipping because of the constant shifts in the cuts and their locations. There were several storm events that instantly sealed one of the cuts and opened another. This created confusion for ship captains who were seeking shelter from open lake storms. As an added source of difficulty, the area near the base of Long Point became an epicenter of land-based pirating (or black-birding, as it was called in Ontario). Under pressure to control Long Point, which was technically owned by England until the time of Canadian Federation, a group of twenty wealthy Canadian and American businessmen purchased the land mass in 1869 and established a controlling entity called the Long Point Company shortly after the Canadian federal government was formed. The new company promised to clean up the illegal activities on the point and added the important promise of aiding the shipping economy by exercising control of the navigational areas and extinguishing the pirating.

Beginning in 1867, the Long Point Company began to take control of the entire Long Point area, including its thousands of acres of interior marshes, savannas and wetlands. The payoff for the company—which consisted of twenty members, half Canadian and half American—was the development of an opulent Long Island–style hunting club in the center of the point that was totally inaccessible from land. Each of the twenty members was given a private cabin for his personal use. To control the expansive peninsula, the Long Point Company created an organization of "keepers" whose job was to patrol both the beaches and the interior of the area and escort unauthorized visitors off the land. This system continued until the 1980s, when the Long Point Company turned the management (but not ownership) of much of the land over to the provincial and federal governments, which began to operate separate wilderness areas. This allowed the Long Point Company to suspend its system of keeper patrols.

Much of the pressure to change the keeper system came from public resentment over the "Millionaires' Club" (a pejorative name), as it was known locally, and was accelerated by the explosion of private boating. So many locals were making unauthorized visits to Long Point that it was impossible to keep people away. As locals were turned away by Long Point Company keepers, the irritation and resentment that was created was a public relations nightmare. The shift from private keepers to provincial and federal authorities, who argued that their role was the preservation of one of North America's last surviving wilderness areas, deflected pressure from the company. As a concession to interest in public use, the Long Point Company, provincial and federal patrols allowed beach access and public use at the tip of the point near the lighthouse and at Pottahawk Point, adjacent to the entrance to the Inner Bay.

One of the joys of being with Dave Stone was that he had a permit to wander the beaches and inland areas of Long Point. He originally used his personal charm and storytelling skills to talk the Long Point Company into the pass. Later, he gained permissions from both the Ontario Provincial and Canadian federal staff, who had set up stations and patrols on Long Point. As a person who had grown up listening to Long Point stories and adventures, I was thrilled to accompany Dave as he wandered the peninsula looking for evidence of shipwrecks.

On one of our first treks to Long Point from Dave's cottage, we pulled his small boat up on the south beach, about five miles from the tip of the point, and began to walk inland over the sand ridges. Cameras in hand, we were hunting for a reported set of ship's ribs that had mysteriously emerged from the sand during a storm. As we walked, we began to hear voices and sounds of digging. After a few minutes, we encountered four men with metal detectors, shovels and picks. They were intently digging in an area that was close to the base of several deciduous trees.

"Treasure hunters," Dave grumbled as we approached.

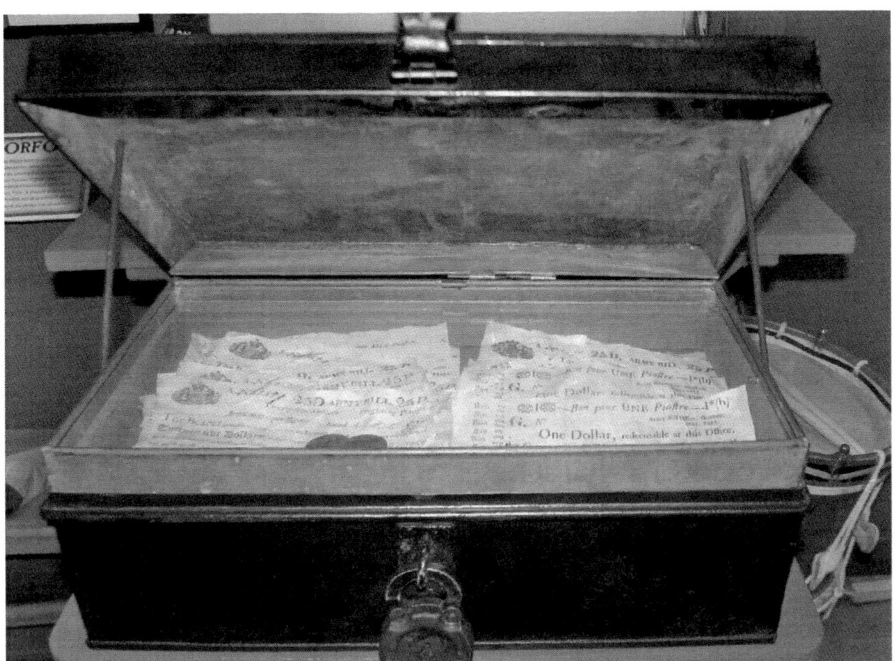

Payroll ship treasure chest exhibit from the Port Dover Harbour Museum. *Courtesy of the Port Dover Harbour Museum.*

When we came closer, they looked at us sheepishly and greeted Dave. "You're Dave Stone, aren't you?" they asked.

"Yup," Dave responded. "Looking for the buried gold?" Dave continued. The foursome grumbled in a confused way as we excused ourselves. As we walked off, Dave looked over his shoulder and added, "You won't find it there."

As we continued our expedition, Dave explained what the foursome was up to. In May 1814, rumors of an impending American naval invasion of the Long Point area permeated Dover Mills and Port Rowan, as well as the local military garrisons. By that time, the September 1813 Battle of Lake Erie had eliminated the protection of the British navy on Lake Erie, and the people who were in charge of the military (militia) in the area were feeling vulnerable.

As persistent rumors of an American invasion began to be replaced by alleged "sightings" of tall ship masts heading for Dover Mills (predecessor of Port Dover), a decision was made to remove the payroll gold and other valuables from the militia bases. To hide the treasure, a small group of militia launched a merchant ship called *Mohawk* and sailed for Long Point. Once they landed, the contingent from Upper Canada's local militia carried the gold inland and buried it in the sand somewhere in the interior. According to legend, the men who buried the gold were sent to the Niagara frontier that summer to fight and never returned.

"Could that be a true story?" I asked.

"What do you think?" Dave answered with a twinkle in his eye.

"What about the alleged boat that was used?" I persisted.

"In those days, the only way a ship became registered and official was when it was captured by the British or Americans and retrofitted for military use," Dave continued. "If the men who buried the treasure used a local trading schooner that had been built by millers or farmers for moving cargo around inside Long Point, there would be no official record of it. So that part of the story is entirely plausible."

Apparently, a lot of people have decided that there might be some truth to the legend of buried gold, as Dave Stone noted that during most years, he encounters at least two such treasure-hunting parties. The typical approach of the stealthy treasure hunters was to anchor a boat near the tip of Long Point, close to the lighthouse, and walk inland with metal detectors. As Dave continued the story, he added that each year, new staff members attached to the provincial and federal outposts on Long Point sit around evening campfires, repeating the old legends of buried treasures. Then they go off with their own metal detectors during their free time.

When I asked Dave if they had ever uncovered anything, his answer was clear and brief: "Empty soup cans!" Now that some years have passed, I still wonder about the legend of buried treasure on Long Point. The last time that I visited the Port Dover Harbour Museum, I noticed that there was an exhibit about it. Must be true!

PART III
OVERLAKE COMMERCE, STEAM AND TECHNOLOGY

THE STEAMSHIP *ERIE* (1841): ERIE'S REED FAMILY

The Reeds were Erie royalty. Dr. Seth Reed moved to Erie from Connecticut in 1795 shortly after the opening of Pennsylvania's new Lake Erie territory to make his fortune on the western frontier. When he arrived, he developed a trading post inside the harbor near the site of the original French Fort, where Erie's largest waterway, Mill Creek, entered Presque Isle Bay. Reed's location was also the northern end of an established trail leading south toward Waterford, Meadville and Pittsburgh. Seth Reed's decision proved brilliant. His competitor, Judah Colt, learned that his two dock locations, while more accessible to sailing ships from the east (Buffalo), suffered from exposure to the open lake. Colt's business also suffered from swampy conditions on the overused trail that led south. The "Low Trail," as it was called in the early days, was subject to flooding and fallen trees.

Seth Reed turned the trading post and hotel over to his son, Rufus, and moved southwest (Colt was southeast), establishing a second location on the "Upper Trail," which connected Erie to points south. That pathway connected with the Lower Trail at Waterford and was generally more passable. The Reed shipping empire began to take shape before the War of 1812, when Rufus lured Daniel Dobbins away from Judah Colt to be the

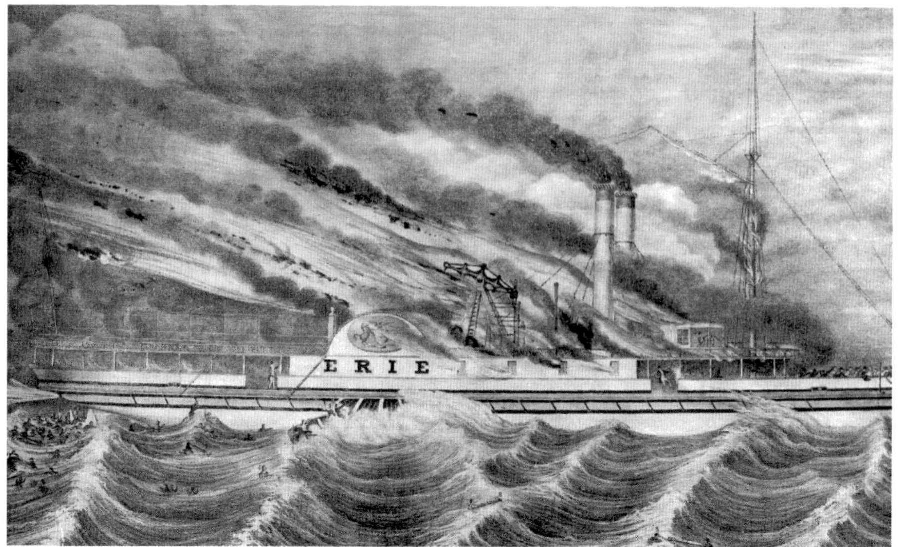

The burning of the steamer *Erie* depicted in a classic lithograph. *Courtesy of Jerry Skrypzak.*

master of a trading schooner. Having a fleet of ships helped the Reeds extend their influence beyond the harbor, and by the first decade of the 1800s, Reed schooners were trading salt for furs in the Georgian Bay. When the war ended, Rufus Reed began to rebuild his fleet with repurposed military ships that had been abandoned when the naval base closed.

The most brilliant Reed business strategist, however, was Rufus's son, Charles Reed, who was sent off for formal education at Washington College and later pursued legal training in Philadelphia (law school was the precursor to today's MBA training). During his time in Philadelphia, one of the largest ports in the United States, Charles could see the coming age of steamships, canals and commerce, as well as the role that the Great Lakes would eventually play in moving goods and people to the West. Things really heated up when Charles Reed returned to take over the family's shipping enterprises. As Rufus shifted his focus to the development of a canal from Erie to the Ohio River west of Pittsburgh, Charles built the largest feet of vessels in the United States. By 1840, the canal to Pittsburgh was bringing passengers and bulk goods back and forth to Pittsburgh, and Charles had carved out a reputation for being the United States' "Steamship King."

To please his upscale wife, Harriet, who was not excited about the prospects of living in a frontier town, Charles hired her brother, Lloyd Gibson, and appointed him chief bursar for the shipping line. Charles's brother-in-law

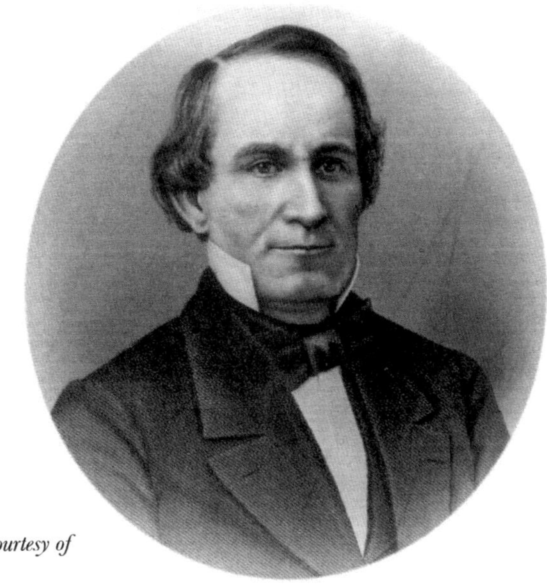

Charles Reed, the steamship king. *Courtesy of Erie County Historical Society.*

was stationed on the company's flagship, the steamer *Erie*. The *Erie* was 176-feet long, displaced 497 gross tons and was launched in Erie in 1836 by master builder Michael Creamer, who was an indirect Reed employee. It was one of the first of Lake Erie's opulent, upper-cabin steamships. While most of the other upper-cabin steamers were owned by railroad companies and served the primary purpose of creating a Lake Erie shortcut from Buffalo to Detroit, the *Erie* ran a regular route between Buffalo and Chicago, making intermediate stops at Erie, Cleveland and Detroit. The steamer *Erie* was special to Charles, who often traveled aboard his favorite ship. The employees of the Reed Shipping Line understood Charles Reed's affection for his flagship and lavished it with high-end features, and the crew was perpetually involved in painting and varnishing.

On August 8, 1841, on a moonlit evening, the *Erie* departed Buffalo with more than three hundred passengers and a cargo packaged in crates and barrels. Its first stop was to be Erie, where Reed's brother-in-law was scheduled to take a few days off. Because the evening originally seemed calm, painters who had been working on the upper decks left several buckets of paint, turpentine and varnish on the deck. As the ship steamed toward Erie through building southwesterly headwinds and waves, the motion became so severe that two members of the Presque Isle Band, which was playing in the main salon, had to excuse themselves and go to the deck because they were seasick. At 8:10

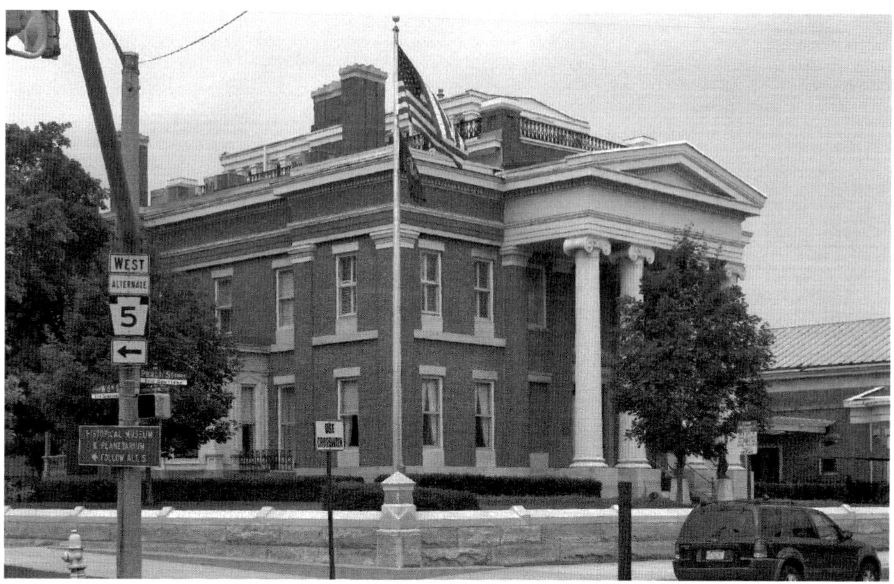

The Reed Mansion, currently home to the downtown Erie Club. *Photograph by Jerry Skrypzak.*

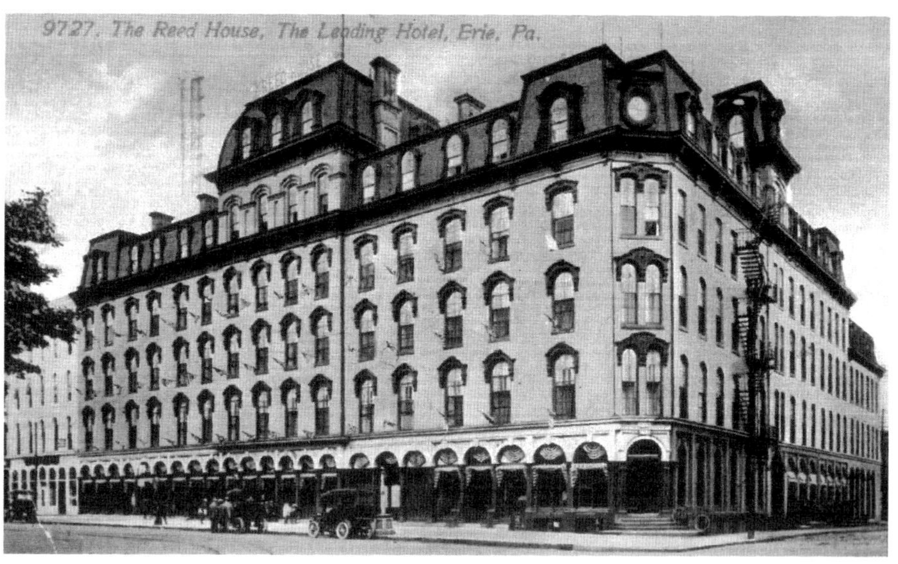

The Reed Hotel in downtown Erie. *Courtesy of Jerry Skrypzak.*

p.m., as the ship was approaching the Pennsylvania state line, the barrels of paint and turpentine on deck were ignited by a spark from the smokestacks. The emergency fire team rushed to the fire, but several of the containers spilled, and within minutes, the fire had spread across the decks. The *Erie* was burning out of control. Captain T.J. Titus ordered the helmsman to steer toward shore and asked him to stay at the wheel for as long as possible. A few miles offshore, however, the steamer *Erie* came to a slow stop. The helmsman, who was later lauded for bravery in several stories and poems, stood by the wheel and guided the ship, which was moving only on momentum, in hopes of running it aground so that passengers and crew could escape. Unfortunately, the *Erie c*ame to a stop more than a mile offshore.

Several steamers spotted the fire and rushed to the rescue, but they were unable to get there in time to save many. As the fire raged out of control and the ship's decks became hotter, passengers and crew took to the water. It was estimated that 200 to 250 people died in the tragic mishap, most of whom were immigrants. One of the deceased was Charles Reed's brother-in-law. While the helmsman (who remained on duty until he had suffered serious burns) was celebrated for his efforts and was reported to have died, Augustus Fuller of Harborcreek, Pennsylvania, later reported that he dove into the water to relieve the burning and that he survived the sinking.

Charles's wife had never been pleased with the prospects of living as a "westerner," as people in the established cities of the East called people in frontier towns like Erie. Even though Erie had grown considerably during the War of 1812, it was still primitive by eastern standards. As of 1841, it had not even received rail service. Mrs. Reed, who imagined herself to have psychic gifts, awoke abruptly from a dream in which her brother was swimming for his life on the evening of the loss. When she learned of the sinking, she was despondent. Unwilling to give up the opportunity to become one of the United States' most successful frontier entrepreneurs, Charles appeased his wife by hiring an architect from Buffalo to build her a home. The resultant mansion, which serves today as the downtown Erie Club, was built between 1846 and 1848 in classic Greek Revival style; at the time of its completion, it was said to be one of the most stunning private residences in America's emerging west.

At the time of his death in 1871, Charles Reed was said to have been the wealthiest man west of New York City. In addition to his business ventures in shipping, banking, the Erie–Pittsburgh canal, a major downtown hotel and railroads, Reed served in the Pennsylvania Congress and held the rank of general in the state militia. His widow remained in the mansion until her death in 1901.

THE SCHOONER *ST. JAMES* (1870): A NEW FLEET MANAGEMENT STRATEGY

After the loss of his flagship, Charles Reed began to rethink the composition of his fleet. At the time of the loss, the Reed Shipping Company fleet consisted of almost forty ships, twenty of which were steam powered. In 1855, Charles Reed announced that he would no longer be adding sail-powered ships to his fleet. He would exclusively be using steamships because that was the way of the future. Between 1850 and 1870, he continued to use his last few structurally sound schooners, but when they returned to Erie each winter for layup, he was increasingly reluctant to spend money on them. He even gave up using the War of 1812 veteran *Caledonia*, his personal favorite, opting to let it languish at his docks.

As of the 1870 season, the *St. James* seemed structurally sound and was sent out for another year of hauling bulk goods. The *St. James* was eighteen years old, having been purchased in Milan, Ohio, in 1852. Rated at 226 gross tons, it was exceptionally large for a sailing schooner, almost twice the size of most Lake Erie sailing ships. The *St. James* typically carried coal west from Reed's Erie docks and returned with grain.

Mysteriously, the *St. James* did not return in the fall of 1870. There were no headlines in the local papers, and the next season, Captain James Burrell, from the *St. James*, was reassigned to another Reed ship. Shipping news was a popular feature of Erie's media, and yet there was no discussion of the old schooner or its whereabouts, which almost certainly meant that there had been no loss of life. Dockside observers surmised that the *St. James* made a late-season delivery and remained in the delivery port for the winter; Reed, who was infamous for ship "horse trading," likely either swapped it for a steamship or sold it.

More than one hundred years later, in 1984, salvage diver Gary Kosak was dragging a modern, side-scan depth sounder across portions of Lake Erie trying to locate the alleged treasure ship *Dean Richmond*. He had assumed that the *Richmond* would be on the bottom of Lake Erie somewhere between Dunkirk, New York, and Erie, but he wondered if it might have been blown north toward Long Point during the storm that consumed it. As he continued to side-scan with the most sophisticated equipment that had ever been used on Lake Erie, he identified several images that were interesting but clearly not the *Dean Richmond*. He carefully recorded the stray images, however, and noted that one, which he found on the

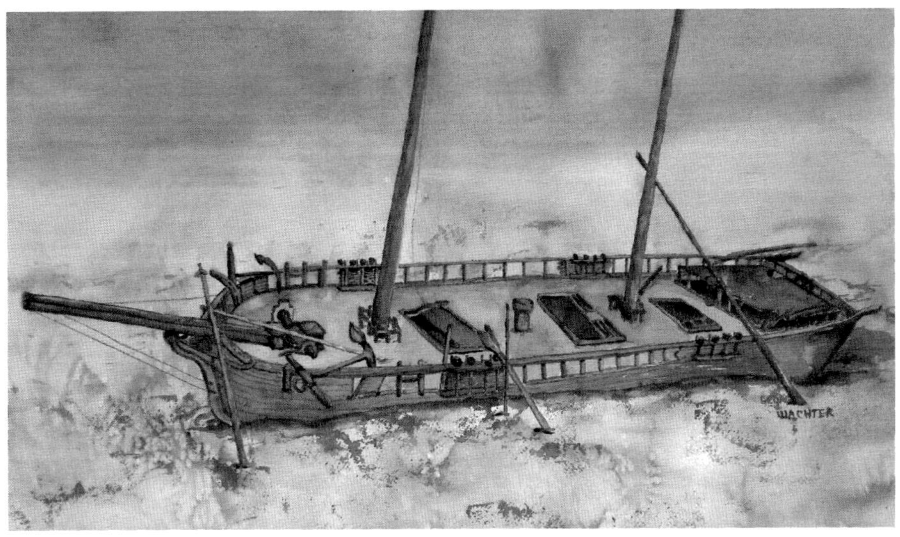

The schooner *St. James* from Erie. *Illustration courtesy of Georgann Wachter.*

south side of Long Point, seemed to be a schooner, approximately one hundred feet in length. Making a note of the LORAN coordinates, Kosak continued on his quest to find the *Dean Richmond.*

Kosak's location tip was passed along to Ontario divers, and by the late 1980s, several had photographed the wreck. It should be noted that relocating such a relatively small target, even with a LORAN location, was not an easy task. Fortunately, once it had been located by locals, it was close enough to shore that divers could use land features to pinpoint it. What they saw when they descended to the 165-foot depths of the mysterious schooner was stunning. The Kosak find was an almost perfectly preserved nineteenth-century schooner lying on the bottom, with its masts still upright and looking as though it could resume its sailing course if it were raised. The extreme depths prevented divers from making a solid identification—thus locals referred to the find as *Mystery Schooner X.* Posters began to appear in Ontario marine stores, and as the fame of the wreck grew, experts converged.

Eventually, marine archaeologists made careful measurements, and their work linked *Mystery Schooner X* to the fall of 1870, when two nearly identical sailing ships sank while eastbound during September and October. Each was built in Ohio by the same yard, 118 feet overall and rated at 226 gross tons. Coincidentally, they were both carrying cargoes of fourteen thousand bushels of wheat. One of the survey divers found a loose hatch board that contained precise tonnage registration numbers. A search of old maritime registries revealed that the numbers as well as the description were a perfect match for the *St. James* from Erie. As more dives were completed, it became apparent that the *St. James* had sunk slowly and probably in calm seas. An inspection of the hold revealed that the load of wheat was permeated with mud, which suggested that the ship had been suffering a slow leak that allowed moisture to invade the hull through faulty oakum calking.

The greatest mystery of the *St. James* was that so little fanfare had accompanied its disappearance. There were a few references to the sinking in Ontario newspapers noting that the ship was American, but there was no publicity on the United States side of Lake Erie. Any hope of using a primary data source was eliminated in the 1940s, when the Reeds, who had shifted their business model from shipping to manufacturing, sold their shipping fleet records to Canadian historian George Cuthbertson. He used the data to publish a number of case studies and papers, but after he passed away in 1969, the records disappeared.

An awareness of Charles Reed's business practices may hold a clue to the fate of the *St. James*. By the time of the loss, the captain and crew of the *St. James* would have been well aware of Reed's distaste for the kinds of disasters that the crew of the steamer *Erie* had suffered. The Reeds preached a strict philosophy of protecting human life after the sinking of the *Erie*.

Slugging along the north shore toward Oswego in a tired wooden ship that was destined to be scrapped, they probably made the decision to abandon their leaking ship, which was not in good enough condition to make any port. Instead of tacking downwind across the open lake, which would have further opened the leaking seams, they probably guided the foundering schooner as close to the base of Long Point as they could and rowed to safety in the lifeboat. From there, they could easily have made their way home. One of the dangers of carrying wheat in the hold of a wooden ship was that if leaking water invaded the cargo, it would cause the grain to swell and put increasing pressure on the seams.

Charles Reed, as the largest shipowner on the Great Lakes, was secretive regarding the composition and movement of his fleet. It would not have been unlike him to receive a call from Captain Burrell of the *St. James* informing him of the loss and then instruct Burrell to come home but keep quiet about the matter. By the next shipping season, the *St. James* was a distant memory in the Reed Yard.

The fortunate outcome of this sinking, which has been characterized as the most well-preserved example of a nineteenth-century sailing ship in existence, is its current state of preservation. If it had not foundered slowly on a relatively calm evening, and sunk slowly in deep water, it would not be there for historians and archaeologists to inspect.

George Mowbray (1880): The Nitro Boat

November is Lake Erie's most fearsome month. The cyclical fall combination of air temperature changes added to rapidly cooling water almost ensures violent storms. November 1880 was particularly nasty, even for the volatile season. Southwest winds built for the first several days of the month and blew almost constantly at twenty to thirty miles per hour for more than a week, churning the lake's surface into a frightening maelstrom. The 1880s were post–Civil War shipping boom years. Railroads were still in their infancy, and the nation was dependent on Great Lakes ships to move materials to the West. But the war effort had taken most of the large, modern Great Lake ships in support of Union war efforts. Lake Erie's remaining fleet was a ragtag assemblage of small, old wooden schooners and freighters, most of which were operating well beyond their designed lives.

By the second week of November, dozens of these ships were docked in Lake Erie ports waiting for a break in the weather. One of them, the two-masted schooner *George Mowbray*, was at Buffalo waiting to depart for Duluth. The cargo was twenty tons of nitroglycerin for use in mining. Nitro was new in those days, and its enormous explosive power was revolutionizing the mining industry. It was also frightening since sailors had little understanding of it. All they knew for sure was that nitro was hundreds of times more powerful than dynamite.

With the shipping season closing in on them, the *Mowbray*'s crew was facing an arduous trip up Lake Erie followed by a long climb up the Detroit and St. Claire Rivers. The *Mowbray*'s captain decided to hitch a ride from Buffalo to Lake Huron with the tug *W.B. Castle*. It was common in those days for specially designed tugs, called "rabbits," to tow schooners upwind to the western end of Lake Erie and/or to haul them up the rivers to Lake Huron, where they would be set free to sail with the prevailing beam wind.

The *W.B. Castle* was contracted to haul one schooner west, so the *Mowbray* hooked on at a reduced rate. Winds and waves eased during the evening of November 9, and at 7:00 a.m., the tug picked up its two tows and left for the

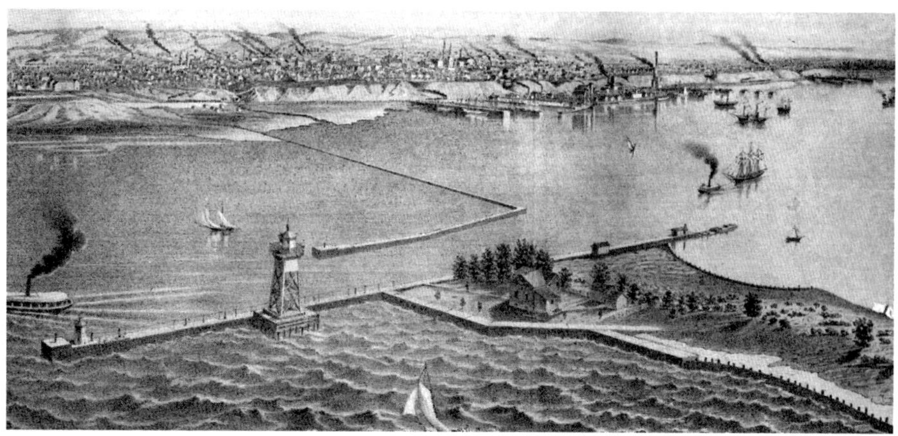

Lithograph of the Erie Harbor, circa 1880. *Courtesy of Jerry Skrypzak.*

Detroit River. It was slow going aboard the double-tow, with speeds averaging only five miles per hour, but the tug could pull the schooners straight up the rumb-line course for the Detroit River, saving the schooners from tacking. At 11:00 a.m., with the *Castle* and its tows only twenty miles west of Buffalo, the wind started to build again, and by 2:00 a.m., the caravan was pounding into thirty-five-mile-per-hour winds and rapidly building seas. The growing waves had slowed the progress of the ships to less than two miles per hour as the tug and its tows slammed into one breaking crest after another.

Meanwhile, crews aboard both the tug and consort schooners were increasingly concerned about the nitroglycerin and how it might react to the pounding waves. At 4:00 p.m., with darkness falling, the captain of the *Castle* decided to abandon his efforts to continue west. There were three possible alternatives. First, they considered cutting *Mowbray* loose so that its crew could sail the schooner back to Buffalo. The downwind run would have eased the pounding and reduced the danger to the cargo, but *Mowbray*'s crew was not particularly anxious to be released in such conditions or to stray from the reassuring presence of the engine-driven *Castle*. For a time, the *Mowbray*'s captain and crew discussed the possibility of abandoning the old schooner in mid-lake and taking refuge on the tug. But the *Castle*'s captain refused, saying that he would not take responsibility for turning a boat full of nitroglycerin loose on Lake Erie.

The other two possibilities both involved running for shelter. They could alter course to the north and head for refuge behind Long Point or try for Erie's harbor. After considering the difficulty of anchoring the tug with its tows behind Long Point, the captain of the *Castle* veered south for Erie. By the time they had made the decision to head for Erie, it was 8:00 p.m. Once the *Castle* changed course, the ship's motion eased considerably, but the winds continued to build as the tug and schooner caravan inched its way toward shelter. By the time they were within sight of Erie, waves had reached twenty to twenty-five feet, and the three-boat roller coaster ride across wave crests had become terrifying.

The crews of the two schooners, even though they were not running sails, were forced to steer constantly to keep their vessels from accelerating down the tops of the waves and overrunning the *Castle* or colliding with one another. The tug would slow its engines as it climbed a wave and then run off the crests and accelerate to avoid being rear-ended by the schooners or fouling its towropes. It was exhausting work, and the specter of a mid-lake collision with a boat full of nitroglycerine caused the crews of all three ships to wonder how anyone could have been stupid enough to have volunteered to haul such a load.

By the time the *Castle* and its tows blew through the Erie Channel on the morning of November 11, all the tug crew could think of was getting rid of the troublesome *Mowbray*. They pulled around the west end of the channel and entered Misery Bay, a recognized storm anchorage. They towed the *Mowbray* as close to the sheltered west bank of the refuge as they could, considering the tug's draft and length of the towrope. Then the captain megaphoned the crew of the *Mowbray* to set anchor and steamed away seeking refuge (with the other schooner still in tow) at the west end of Presque Isle Bay.

As the *Mowbray* anchored to ride out the storm, the captain and crew realized that they would be on their own for the rest of the trip. There was no way that the *Castle* was going to come back for them or continue towing the nitro boat. After more than twenty-four hours of nerve-racking pounding aboard a floating bomb (as they later characterized the *Mowbray*), the captain and crew found the anchor slipping in an ice-cold rainstorm. Then, as they contemplated their options, the circumstances deteriorated. The anchor that they had set was much too far from the sheltering western shore of Misery Bay, and as winds and waves continued to build, the schooner began to yaw violently from side to side. By 1:00 p.m. on the afternoon of November 11, the anchor was dragging, and the schooner was being pushed east across Misery Bay. The crew made a number of attempts to stop the ship, finally resorting to raising a sail in the hope of sailing away to the west end of Presque Isle Bay, where the *Castle* was anchored. But they had waited too long. When the sail went up, the wind caught the schooner and pushed it even faster toward the east.

Seeing that the ship was out of control, the captain tried desperately to steer it aground on the beach, but winds and waves overpowered the ship. *Mowbray* washed up against a row of wooden pilings that guarded the open end of Misery Bay from the channel entrance. The old schooner eventually snagged on the pilings, hung up, listed to starboard and began to pound violently. Each wave was propelling the bow and then the stern up against the wooden stakes. Within minutes, the *Mowbray*'s starboard rail had fractured, boards were separating from the hull and the old schooner was taking on water. Ultimately, the starboard rail collapsed so that *Mowbray*'s bow and stern were both caught on the pilings. That was the end for the old schooner. As the waves continued, the *Mowbray* listed violently to starboard one last time and began to sink.

The crew at Erie's lifesaving station had been keeping an eye on the *Mowbray*, and as the men watched, they were surprised to see the captain and crew launch a lifeboat, leap aboard carrying personal belongings in sea bags and row to shore. It was clear that they were abandoning ship, but the watchmen could only guess the reasons until the exhausted, bedraggled and frightened sailors reported the circumstances of the ship and cargo.

Shipping news reporters were ravenous for stories about ships and shipwrecks, especially during the fall. When the media learned about the *Mowbray* after interviewing near-hysterical crew members as well as the lifesaving station crew, they ratcheted the dangers of the nitro boat to frightening proportions (there were no local technical experts to help interpret the actual danger). By the time the November 12 papers hit the stands, headlines read, "Nitro Boat Loose in The Bay: Erie's East Side to Be Evacuated."

Fortunately, not many of Erie's seasoned east siders abandoned their homes. While the newspapers reported that Erie's East Side neighborhoods could be "leveled" at any moment, residents hunkered down and hoped for the best. St. Patrick's Church held a prayer vigil, schools canceled classes and bay-front locals refused to allow their children to leave home.

On November 15, the wind and waves calmed, and several commercial fishermen bravely took it on themselves to rescue the town. They led a contingent of volunteers with two tugboats to Misery Bay, where they made a daylong attempt to free the *Mowbray* and move it to a secure anchorage away from the pilings. The schooner was too far gone to be rescued, however, so they abandoned their efforts and towed the foundering remains of the

Mowbray into the shallows, where it was run aground. The next day, the men returned with a scow borrowed from the Erie Sand & Gravel Company, waded to the *Mowbray* in ice-cold water and spent the morning unloading the fifty-pound packing crates filled with nitroglycerin, which were then placed on the scow. By this time, the owner of the cargo had sent assurances via telegraph that the nitroglycerin, once secured and stored in an outdoor location, would be quite safe.

The cargo's owner arranged for the steamer *Georgian*, from Port Ryerse, Ontario (just across the lake from Erie and west of Port Dover), to continue the shipment. The *Georgian* arrived at Misery Bay on November 21, offloaded the nitro from the beached barge and began steaming up Lake Erie for the Detroit River and Lake Superior. But the owner/captain of the *Georgian* had not been entirely honest about the cargo when he recruited a last-minute crew for this late-season run. He was anxious to earn the shipping fee for one final run and felt that his steamer had plenty of time to get to Duluth and back before winter closed in on them. But the crew from Erie's lifesaving station was on hand to supervise the transfer of the nitroglycerin, and they shared the scary stories about the troubled cargo with *Georgian*'s sailors. The troubling stories quickly caused a wave of discontent among crew members, and by the time they had steamed an hour into Lake Erie, the frightened Ontario crew had convinced their captain that they were heading on a suicide mission.

Convinced that the load was jinxed, the captain reluctantly agreed to give up his plans and take the load to Port Colborne instead. There, he reasoned, the nitroglycerin could be unloaded and placed in a warehouse. It also seemed that Port Colborne would be a more prudent destination since it was downwind and the weather was worsening again. But the nitroglycerin cargo seemed to have a will of its own. As soon as the captain altered course for Port Colborne, *Georgian*'s engine failed, leaving the old ship floating at the mercy of Lake Erie. A day later, *Georgian*'s crew spotted a tug steaming east. They signaled for assistance, and the tug, which was returning from a tow up the Detroit River, passed a line to the steamer and towed it to Buffalo. On November 24, exactly two weeks after the nitroglycerin had left Buffalo Harbor, it unceremoniously returned to its point of origin.

The *Georgian* sat deteriorating in Buffalo Harbor for several years before it was scrapped. The splintered remains of the *Mowbray* were towed to the middle of Misery Bay and scuttled the next spring in the same general location as the sunken remains of the *Lawrence* and *Niagara*. The nitroglycerin was ultimately shipped west by railroad.

Norwegian Angst (1852): Touched by a Shipwreck

Bruce Weaver is a typical, upper-middle-class North Carolinian whose great-grandparents left Norway in the mid-1800s and made their way to Wisconsin. There were family stories about a shipwreck and an old multi-page, yellowed document that his maternal great-grandmother had painstakingly written in Norwegian. The treasured papers had been entrusted to Bruce, and he safeguarded them for decades. The word *Atlantic* was repeated, but he assumed that it was a reference to Great-Grandmother Marit's arduous trip across the Atlantic Ocean. Then, on a remarkable Sunday in 2008, a temporary summer minister came to Bruce's Lutheran Church in Greensboro, North Carolina. The young preacher was a delightful transplant from Norway who spoke both English and Norwegian. After meeting the minister, Bruce thought of his great-grandmother's journal and took it to him.

The story that emerged after the translation was so moving that the minister and an archivist who was contacted from the Norwegian-American Historical Society were stunned. The journal was a narration of the determination and bravery of a woman who had survived the sinking of the steamer *Atlantic* in Lake Erie en route to Wisconsin on an odyssey that modern people would find unbelievable.

Marit née Hove was born in Vestre Slidre, Norway, in 1813. In 1845, she married Ole Rodvang and then struggled to make a living on a farm where they had two children. Things were difficult in Scandinavia during the time of the Irish potato famine. Norwegian farms had experienced decades of bumper crops, infant and child mortality had fallen and since the population was growing faster than economic opportunities, the Rodvangs (along with thousands of other Norwegians) decided to make their way to North America. There was a man in their town named Steven Olsen who offered immigration services. For a fee, Olsen led groups across the Atlantic, through the complexities of immigration and then to Wisconsin, where his charges would be connected with established Norwegian settlers.

Marit's husband, Ole, and his three brothers—Finkel, Barbo and Knud—all paid to leave Norway together. They departed Vestre Slidre in November 1851, stopping in the neighboring towns of Vang, Aurdal and Toten to add to Olsen's group of nearly one hundred. Travelers were told to pack one steamer trunk per family with clothing, food for the trip and essentials for their new lives in North America. They were also advised

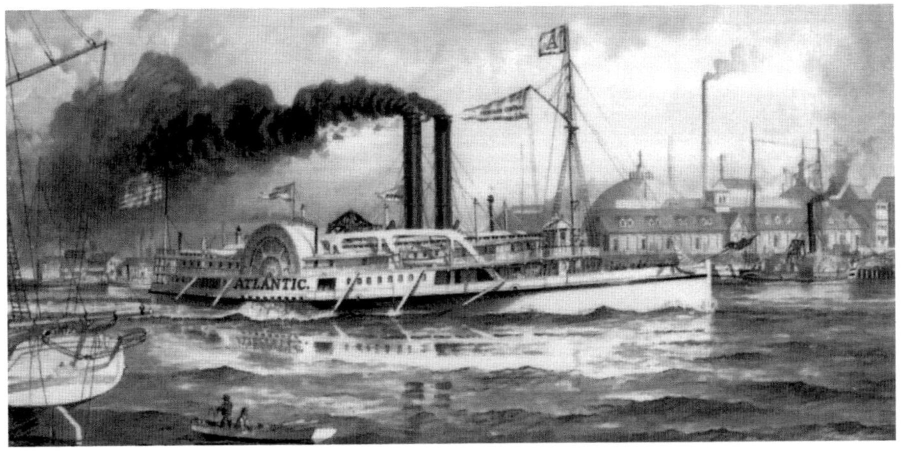

The steamer *Atlantic. Illustration by Robert McGreevy and courtesy of the Port Dover Harbour Museum.*

to bring enough money to cover both transatlantic sailing tickets and transportation costs for the trip across North America.

An extremely difficult winter presented the first glitch. On the first leg of the trip to Norway's seaport of Drammen, snow and mud slowed the progress of their wagons, and the group arrived a day late, missing connections. They purchased tickets for the crossing on another ship, but they had to wait in Drammen for nine weeks because their ship, the *Argo*, had to be returned to dry-dock in England for repairs. The *Argo* was a sloop-rigged lumber hooker that had been "round steeled" to make the hull last longer. Spring storms delayed *Argo*'s return to Drammen, and the ship's captain sent word to Steven Olsen that if the Norwegians wanted to leave, they would have to meet the ship in the port of Christiana, another two-week trip. Since they had purchased tickets, they had little choice. By late June, when the party finally boarded and set off for America, it had spent more of its limited resources than it had planned.

Any hope of a fast crossing evaporated when the Norwegians, who had been sandwiched into a tiny below-deck cargo hold, saw how clumsy the *Argo* was in the open seas. The five-year-old ship's heavy, metal-encapsulated hull caused it to suffer a painfully slow speed through the water. To make matters worse, the waterline length of only 58.9 feet and relatively narrow beam of 14.4 feet made it wallow in the massive North Atlantic waves. And if the below-deck crowding had not been uncomfortable enough, eight weeks of tedious rolling through waves made things miserable. But the Norwegians were tough. Even though there were bouts of nausea, vomiting and diarrhea, no one died on the crossing, a remarkable achievement given the crowded, wet conditions. When the crew sounded the "land ho" signal in the Gulf of St. Lawrence, Steven Olsen led his party of Norwegians in traditional Lutheran prayers of thanksgiving.

Marit Rodvang was so happy to disembark the crowding and stench of the *Argo* that she didn't care that they had not landed at their anticipated port of New York. Olsen was concerned, however, since he was not as experienced with transportation systems in Quebec. Undaunted, he led his party toward Buffalo, where he planned to book passage for Detroit. It took two weeks of train and wagon rides, but on the second week of August, almost eight months after leaving their homes, the bedraggled group finally arrived in Buffalo, where Olsen had Norwegian connections. Sadly, the long travel delays had been costly, and many of Olsen's party members did not have enough money left to purchase steamer tickets to Detroit at the docks of the Ward Steamship Company. Olsen arranged for the seventy "unlucky" travelers (who were out of money) to be taken in by Buffalo's Norwegian community before departing with thirty-four on August 20, 1852. For Marit Rodvang and her family, who were among those who continued, the promise of a new life in Milwaukee seemed just a few short days away.

After a frustrating six-hour wait at the docks while food, supplies and first- and second-class passengers were being boarded, the Norwegians were led down into the cavernous below-deck steerage quarters of the steamer *Atlantic* while their trunks were taken aboard the great ship. The Rodvangs were surprised and delighted to see how beautiful and ornate the *Atlantic* was in comparison to the *Argo*. The *Atlantic* was fresh and clean, and as the Norwegians descended into the dark steerage space, they could hear happy sounds of upper-deck passengers enjoying the beautiful summer evening. Smells of fine cooking permeated the soft evening air. Marit was sorry to be going below since it was such a lovely evening, but she was anxious to settle down for the evening and find a place where her two exhausted children could rest. The trip to Detroit was said to be easy, smooth and fast. The only concerns that had reverberated through the crowds at the pier were stories of Lake Erie storms and steamship fires. On the positive side, there would be no waiting for wind or rolling from side to side in huge North Atlantic waves, and Marit's husband, Ole, assured her that the rumors of fires aboard Lake Erie steamships were exaggerated. The steamer *Erie* had burned on Lake Erie a few years earlier, but that fire could have been prevented by simple safety precautions, and Olsen assured his charges that safety had improved.

By 11:00 p.m., the steady motion of the *Atlantic* and hypnotic rumbling of the ship's paddle wheels had lulled the entire Rodvang family to sleep. They had secured a place near an interior bulkhead, and both their daughter, Ambjer, and two-year-old son, Ole, were fast asleep. All seemed perfect for the sleepy family until Marit suddenly awoke to a terrible crunching sound and violent forward lurch. The impact of a collision literally threw the sleeping steerage crowd across the hold of the ship, piling people onto one another. Within minutes, children were screaming, while sleepy mothers and fathers were furtively attempting to restore order. Marit scrambled across the chaos of strewn passengers searching for her two children. She had the most trouble locating her son, who had been thrown the farthest because he was small. It had not dawned on Marit that the ship was in serious difficulty. In the cacophony of spoken Norwegian, German, Swedish and Irish, the steerage passengers were desperately trying to organize families. Marit tried to find Steven Olsen, but he was nowhere to be seen.

Concern that the *Atlantic* had collided with something and was going to sink began to circulate, and then rumors erupted: "The *Atlantic* had struck a reef." "No! It had pulled into a port to take on supplies and rammed the docks." Then the paddle wheels began to move, and the ship was underway. Someone said that the ship's wheel had simply hit a submerged log. Just when things seemed to be returning to normal, however, the forward end of the boat began to sink. People were sliding toward the bow and finding it difficult to gain footing. Finally, a cloud of steam and smoke billowed through the steerage compartments, and panic began in earnest. A frantic rush of humanity began to press uphill toward the stern. Marit and Ole gripped their children, struggled to keep their footing and tried not be trampled.

The doors to the decks opened, but even though the ship's stewards were yelling instructions, no one could hear or understand what they were saying since they were in English. Steven Olsen appeared for a brief moment, shouting for the party to stay together and remain calm, but before he could make himself understood, he was swept away by an avalanche of people. Ole held on to their daughter, and Marit lifted their son, clutching him to her chest. The ship was lurching forward, apparently diving bow first toward the bottom of Lake Erie.

As Ole gathered his family and herded them away from the panicked mob on deck, the sight that greeted the Rodvangs was frightening. Billowing clouds of steam and smoke surrounded the once opulent ship, and the bow was sinking rapidly. Meanwhile, panicked immigrants were leaping into the water, where many disappeared, never to return. Shrieks and moans punctuated the evening air, conveying a common human language that did not have to be translated.

Then Ole noticed something strange. The first- and second-class passengers from the upper decks seemed unusually calm. Their demeanor made Ole hesitate to follow in the footsteps of the Norwegians who were leaping into the water and fighting over bits of flotsam. The upper-cabin American passengers were moving toward the stern rather than jumping overboard.

"This way," Ole urged Marit. He and his wife ushered the children away from the mêlée and toward the stern, in the opposite direction from which the steerage class passengers were moving. After several steps, however, the Rodvangs came to a moment of decision. The *Atlantic* was steadily pitching forward, and as it did, water was rising to meet them on the deck.

"We need to get into the water and away from the boat," Ole whispered to his wife. Picking up a stool that had been discarded by an upper-class passenger, he grabbed Ambjer and slipped over the side rail. Testing the stool's buoyancy, he pressed his daughter between himself and the float and then pleaded for his wife to join him in the water. "Quick, before others come and take our stool away!" he urged her. "I'm sure that it will hold all of us."

Marit was a dutiful wife, and every fiber of her being wanted to do as her husband had instructed, but she could not swim. She had always been terrified by water. Unlike Ole, Marit had never learned to swim. If she were to release her grip on the *Atlantic*, she feared that her two-year-old son would die. As Ole and Ambjer drifted away, Marit found her way to the hogging-arches that guarded the *Atlantic*'s paddle wheel and fought for a handhold. Gripping little Ole in one hand, she allowed herself to float upward along the arches and on the edge of the paddle wheel while the bow slowly sunk. Eventually, she grasped a piece of steel bracing attached to the smokestack, and it was there that she held on with the ferocity of a mother whose only mission was to save the life of her son—a death grip.

After two desperate hours of clinging to the side of the *Atlantic* and trying to calm her son, the steamer *Ogdensburg* came alongside and began taking upper-class passengers and crew from the stern. Marit screamed for help, trying to attract attention, but her voice didn't seem to have any volume. No one responded. Then, just as she was afraid that her grip would fail, a strong hand circled her waist and lifted her to safety with her son. Her savior was the *Atlantic*'s bursar, Julius Morvine, the last person to leave the ship. When she finally reached the safety of the *Ogdensburg*, Marit was overjoyed to find Ole and Ambjer aboard as well.

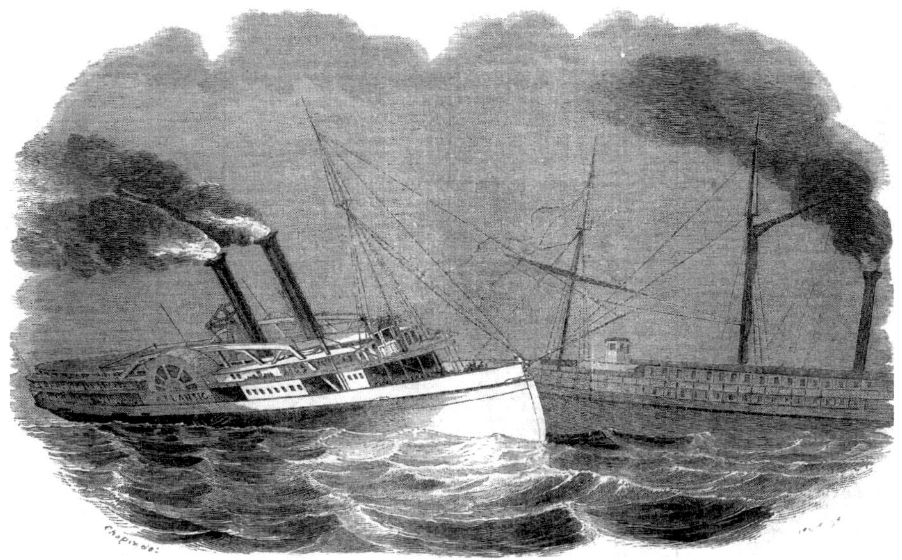

The *Atlantic* colliding with the eastbound steamer *Ogdensburg*. *Courtesy of the Norway Heritage Collection, www.norwayheritage.com; source: www.heritage-ships.com.*

Eight hours later, the *Ogdensburg*, overloaded with two hundred rescued passengers and crew, limped into Erie, Pennsylvania. Of Steven Olsen's party of Norwegians, sixty-eight had perished. The drowning victims included two of Ole's brothers, Finkel and Barbo, both of their wives and their four small children. The rescued Norwegians landed in Erie with only the wet clothing that they were wearing. Their steamer trunks containing the food, clothing and supplies needed to begin new lives in Wisconsin had gone to the bottom.

The next portion of the Rodvangs' odyssey may have been even more remarkable in terms of psychological bravery. The survivors boarded the steamer *Sultana* and returned to Buffalo, where they were placed aboard the *Mayflower*, sister ship of the *Atlantic*, for another try at the Lake Erie run to Detroit. If they had not been out of money, starving, cold and without clothing, they would never have allowed themselves to be reboarded on another steamship. In Detroit, a charitable group fed and clothed the Norwegians and sponsored their fare on a train for Milwaukee.

On September 26, ten months after leaving Norway, Ole and Marit Rodvang finally arrived in Koshkonog, Wisconsin. Ole and Marit lived a quiet, rural life, ultimately moving from Wisconsin to Iowa and raising their two children. Marit's husband, Ole, passed away in 1884, and Ambjer, the daughter who had been saved from the tragic sinking, was trampled to death by a bull in 1900. Marit learned to speak English but could only write in Norwegian. She and Ole insisted that their children learn to read and write English, and consequently, when she passed the journal containing the story of her immigration experiences to Ambjer, her daughter was never able to understand it. Ambjer and her brother, Ole, had only vague recollections of their trip from Norway to Wisconsin. Marit Rodvang died peacefully in 1902 at age eighty-nine.

The sacrifices of the Rodvangs were typical of North American immigrants: leaving home, never to return, and cutting ties with family and friends. Is it any wonder that the collective psychological experiences of people like the Rodvangs has resulted in a powerful ethnic angst, a pervasive genetically imprinted expectation of trial, tribulation and suffering? To Ambjer, who passed her mother's Norwegian journal along to her own daughter before she died in 1900, and her grandson, Bruce Weaver, we are grateful for this glimpse into the immigrant experience.

SALVAGING THE STEAMER *ATLANTIC*: JOHNNY GREEN DISCOVERS THE BENDS

On a calm August evening in 1852, one of Lake Erie's opulent, upper-cabin steamships left Buffalo for Detroit with a full complement of packaged goods, about four hundred immigrants heading for the West and an array of first- and second-class passengers. Nothing about the evening would have seemed dangerous. While there was a surface haze, the moon and stars shone brightly through a dark sky, and first-class passengers enjoyed luxury meals, the ship's orchestra and dancing in the upper salons. Suddenly, near Long Point, there was a terrible grinding collision as the *Atlantic* unexplainably collided with the eastbound *Ogdensburg*.

The two ships separated almost immediately and the *Atlantic*'s captain assumed that the damage was minimal, but it soon became apparent that the grand steamship was going down. The captain tried a desperate run for the shore of Long Point, where he hoped to save the ship by running it aground, but he did not make it. Within an hour, the *Atlantic* was settling bow-first into the deepest portion of Lake Erie, and the *Ogdensburg* had returned to try to recover passengers and crew.

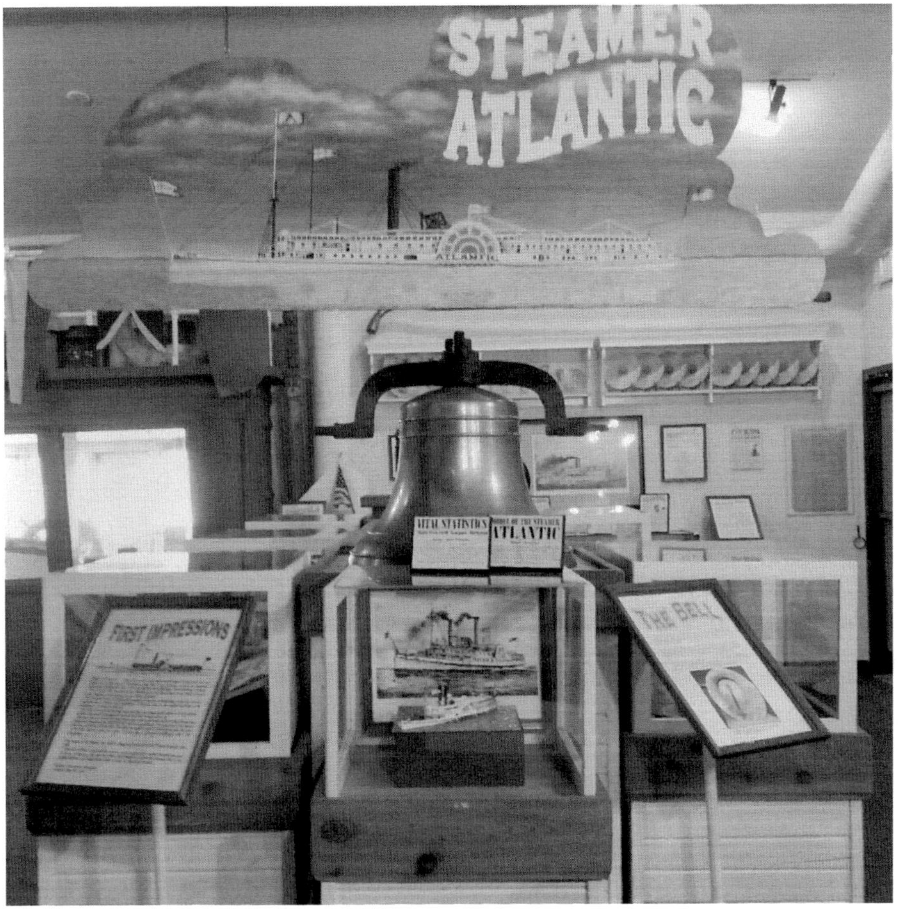

The steamer *Atlantic* collection at the Port Dover Harbour Museum. *Courtesy of Port Dover Harbour Museum.*

One of the most interesting aspects of the collision was connected to a business decision. The American Express Company was experimenting with the transport of gold, cash and other valuables to the Northwest Territories in a safe aboard the *Atlantic*. The decision was controversial, and the two men who argued for it, Henry Wells and William Fargo, had convinced the board of directors that since the railroads had been unable to lay track along the south shore of Lake Erie, steamships would provide the most efficient transit. From the perspective of American Express, the loss of two hundred to three hundred lives (an accurate count was never confirmed) and the steamship, while tragic, was secondary to losing the company safe on its inaugural passage.

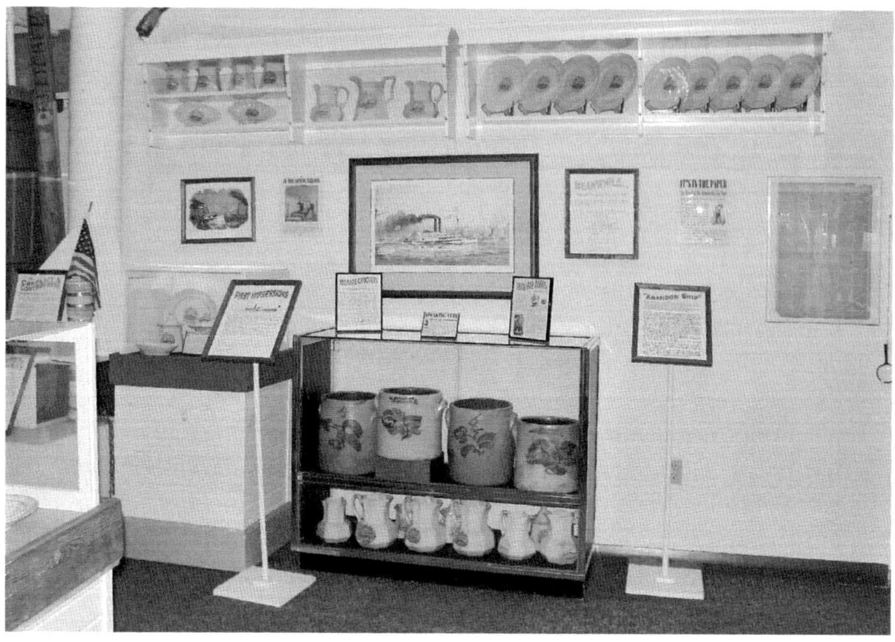

These artifacts, preserved by Mike Fletcher, were more valuable to the history of immigration than the treasures imagined by profit-oriented salvers. *Photograph by Mary Ann Frew.*

Wells and Fargo hired Johnny Green, a well-known salvage diver from upstate New York, to recover the safe. Its agent aboard the *Atlantic*, who survived the sinking, had clearly marked the safe's location as the ship went down, and Wells and Fargo passed that information to Green, along with a description of the location of the sunken ship that had been kept a secret. The company also provided a misguided report that the ship was lying in less than one hundred feet of water. Responding to the lure of a major salvage fee, Green immediately departed for Port Dover, the closest port to the wreck site.

On his first descent, he was troubled to learn that the actual depth was closer to 170 feet, well beyond any previous salvage attempts. Undaunted, however, he continued to dive to the *Atlantic* and adjust, repair and replace equipment that was failing as he dove. When his patched-together pumps and air hoses finally allowed him to descend all the way to the deck of the *Atlantic*, he found the safe, chopped away at cabin structure, which separated it from the open deck, and managed to drag it out, where he attached a line. As he was making his deep dives, however, Johnny Green was growing sicker and sicker. After his final descent, just before he planned to add a safety line and retrieve the safe, he staggered across the deck of the salvage boat and collapsed. His crew took him to Port Dover, where the town doctor concluded that there was no way to save him.

There had been preliminary research on the diving sicknesses associated with changes in atmospheric pressure, but at the time of Johnny Green's collapse, there was no name or clear understanding of the malady that is now known as the "bends." In fact, diving sickness was not given a proper name until bridge builders, particularly on the Brooklyn Bridge project more than twenty years later, named it "caisson disease." That name emerged because it seemed to be a malady of workers who were one atmosphere or more under the water's surface (approximately thirty-three feet) anchoring bridge footings from inside submerged steel caissons. The chief engineer of the Brooklyn Bridge Project, Washington Roebling, suffered from the disease for the rest of his life and was permanently disabled as a result of his time working in bridge caissons.

The difference between Johnny Green's exposure and that of the bridge and mine workers who had experienced similar problems was that his exposure was brief and severe, while those of the caisson workers were gradual and extended. Prior to Johnny Green, there were no records of divers experiencing such illnesses.

Johnny Green semi-recovered in Port Dover, and then he went home to New York State to convalesce. Convinced that the safe would be waiting on the deck of the *Atlantic*, he returned the next season. Green descended to the ship himself since he could find no one else willing to do the dive, but he found that the safe was gone. He later learned that one of his diving crew, Elliot Harrington from Dunkirk, New York, had returned a few weeks before he did in 1853 and made off with the safe. Harrington tried to deny that he had done it, but the trail of evidence was too compelling for him to get away with his plot. American Express settled with Harrington and recovered the safe with most of its contents. Johnny Green never completely recovered from his diving sickness. He spent the rest of his life crippled and angry and passed away prematurely from his injuries.

A number of others seemed to have been forever touched by the events of the *Atlantic* sinking. Wells and Fargo left American Express and started its own specialized transport company. The familiar Wells Fargo stagecoaches that delivered payroll monies and other important valuables to the emerging West had their roots in Lake Erie's sinking of the *Atlantic*. Other early salvage divers visited the *Atlantic*, including the inventor of one of North America's early submarines. Lodner Philips, from Michigan City, Indiana, was trying to sell his invention to the United Sates Navy for use in the Civil War. He dove at the site of the *Atlantic* to publicize his invention but lost his prototype submarine near the site of the *Atlantic*; he also failed to win a navy contract. The unnamed Philips diving machine has never been located.

During the mid-1980s, Port Dover diver Mike Fletcher rediscovered the location of the sunken *Atlantic* and made a protracted attempt to salvage and preserve it while working with the Port Dover Harbour Museum. His efforts received international attention when a salvage diving group from the United States called Mar Dive challenged his "ownership" of the wreck and its contents. While Mike was intent on telling the story of the *Atlantic* and preserving its historically significant artifacts at the town museum, Mar Dive sold shares in the venture, claiming that the *Atlantic* contained untold treasures. After a protracted Toronto court battle, the conflict was settled in favor of Mike and the Province of Ontario, and the collection is currently housed at Port Dover's Harbour Museum.

DEAN RICHMOND (1893): SALVAGE DIVING PRECEDENTS

The first time I visited Dave Stone at his Long Point cottage, I was greeted by an amazing assortment of shipwreck relics. The exterior of his place was jammed with flotsam, jetsam and schooner parts. Winter poles, buoys, fishnet markers and wooden ship's ribs seemed to be growing like garden weeds between Dave's garage and the walkway to his cottage, and inside there were even more ship's parts. Dave's wife, Jean, joked that she lived at a marine salvage yard rather than in a cottage.

When I expressed amazement, Dave laughed and took me on a quick field trip to the Backus Preservation Center a few miles away. "Should have seen my cottage a few years ago," he joked. "Since then, I have donated almost everything to Backus," he added.

When we arrived, we visited an exhibit aptly named Davey Stones Locker, which was filled with pieces that he had donated. "Jean was the happiest woman in the world when we got rid of the stuff that is in this museum," Dave laughed. "I used to be like all the divers," he continued as we toured the exhibit. "If I found a shipwreck, I felt that I had to take something. It was commonplace for divers to remove souvenirs from shipwrecks that they found in the old days," he added." They would start with removable pieces like hardware, cleats, winches, anchors and bollards. Then, as the wrecks became picked over, they would use tools to pry boards and other structural pieces loose."

"What did they do with all the stuff?" I asked.

"Lacking an understanding of the proper ways to preserve such items, especially the wood bits, souvenirs were propped up on mantels or hung on walls until chemical changes in the newly brought-to-the-surface wood eroded the very pieces that had once served as beloved trophies," he responded. "Lots of it ended up in dumpsters."

"Nobody does that anymore," he continued, "and I for one am embarrassed by the way I used to remove things. That was the real reason that I donated everything to this museum, where curators know how to preserve and care for artifacts. Everything changed in the world of shipwrecks and diving in 1984 when a salvage diver found the *Dean Richmond* near Erie," he offered. "Now the only things that I collect are pieces that wash up on the beach."

Dave continued by telling the story of how the *Dean Richmond* changed diving ethics. In 1893, a wooden package freight steamer named *Dean Richmond* left Cleveland for Buffalo with a cargo of flour, lead and zinc ingots. The *Richmond*, which was launched in 1864, had a reputation for being a "bad-luck ship" by virtue of four near disasters and an 1871 sinking. The twin-propeller ship was raised after it went down in the St. Mary's River and then was towed to Buffalo, rebuilt and put back into service in 1873. To add to the specter of the ship's bad luck, the *Dean Richmond* departed Cleveland in October 1893 on Friday the thirteenth, in defiance of a longstanding maritime tradition that would have frowned on such a thing.

As Captain G.W. Stoddard headed east, he found himself in a typical Lake Erie October squall, a storm that raged for more than three days, with winds that were registered at a sustained fifty miles per hour and huge breaking waves. Observers estimated the wave crests at more than twenty-five feet. To make matters worse, Stoddard was heading along shore, where the breakers would have been the most dangerous.

Bodies and bits of the cargo began to wash on shore east of Dunkirk, New York, and this convinced many that the ship had sunk in mid-lake close to the Pennsylvania/New York border. All eighteen crew members eventually washed ashore, as did the ship's lifeboat. One crew member was alive when he was found, but he died later of exposure. In addition to bodies and a lifeboat, debris from the ship and barrels of flour were recovered for weeks.

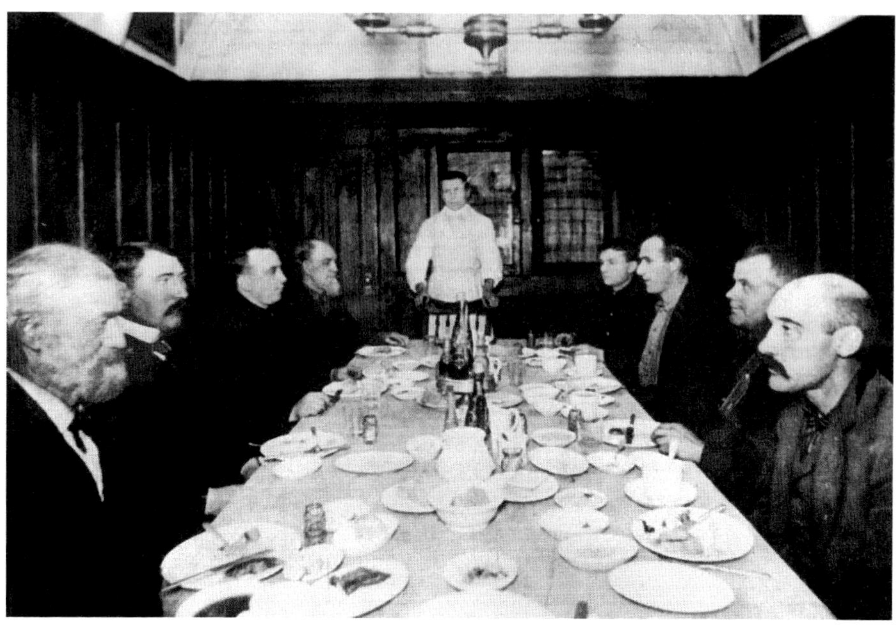

The crew of the *Dean Richmond*. *Courtesy of Jerry Skrypzak.*

The search for the *Dean Richmond* was confused by the location of the debris field, which stretched for miles east of Dunkirk. The debris field convinced searchers that the ship would be found offshore in New York State. In 1975, salvage diver Gary Kosak returned to the Great Lakes after time spent diving in support of the offshore drilling industries in Canada and Mexico and began to hunt for the *Dean Richmond.* Using modern side-scan sonar, he relentlessly continued for nine years before he found it. His final discovery, after serendipitously locating dozens of other wrecks on the bottom of Lake Erie, surprised everyone, including himself. The wooden steamer was lying just off North East (Freeport), Pennsylvania, in 105 feet of water, miles from where it was expected and much closer to Erie than anyone had imagined.

While there had been rumors that the *Dean Richmond* was carrying gold and other valuables, Kosak's summer 1984 salvage operation revealed nothing more than the official lead and zinc ingots that had been listed as part of the original manifest. Gary Kosak worked from Erie as he salvaged the *Dean Richmond*, and as he did, he raised a furor of controversy by using dynamite to blast a hole in the hull to make it easier to move about and bring cargo to the surface.

The ship lies upside down on the bottom, with its inverted hull reaching to within seventy feet of the lake surface. Novice divers can easily descend to within camera range of the inverted hull, while the more experienced and daring often enter through the hole provided by Kosak so they can swim through the interior.

Perhaps the most important impact of Kosak's work, however, was the eventual tightening of underwater dive rules. Within a few years of his salvage operation, the Province of Ontario and the four American states on the south side of Lake Erie (Michigan, New York, Ohio and Pennsylvania) enacted strict regulations encouraging divers to look at but not touch underwater wrecks. Ontario later added a regulation making it illegal to descend beyond thirty meters without a hard-hat rig and surface-provided air supply.

Marquette & Bessemer No. 2 (1909): Still Missing After All These Years

Word spread like wildfire on Sunday, December 10, 1909: A recovered lifeboat! Gruesome dead bodies! People came by the hundreds, wandering down Erie's State Street, where they jockeyed for position to see one of the most macabre visions in the city's history. Eight dead men were sitting upright in a twenty-foot lifeboat. A ninth was curled into a fetal position under a block of ice that extended to the gunnels. The bodies were frozen solid in waist-deep ice. While authorities struggled to free the frozen crew, the crowd pressed forward to glimpse the awful sight. Families watched in horror. Mothers chided children. "Stay away from the water." "Never become sailors."

Finally, an enterprising policeman thought of a way to free the frozen bodies. The lifeboat was gingerly towed to the dock where the USS *Michigan* (later renamed *Wolverine*) was stationed. A hose was connected between the *Michigan*'s steam exhaust outlet and the lifeboat's scupper. Then, slowly, as hot exhaust water bubbled through the lifeboat, the block of ice that had encapsulated the sailors melted away.

Two of the most haunting images in local maritime history were featured in local newspapers that week. A photograph of Captain Jeremy Driscoll, from the Pennsylvania Fish Commission, standing next to the lifeboat, and a coroner's photograph of the nine deceased men on preparation tables at Hanley's Funeral Home.

The Erie portion of the great adventure of 1909 began on Thursday, December 7, when Albert Weis left the train station for Conneaut, Ohio. Weis was corporate treasurer of Curtze Industries and chief operating officer of Keystone Fish. In those days, Curtze was a diversified business involved in steel, locomotive manufacturing and commercial fishing. Weis was en route to Port Stanley, Ontario, representing Curtze's Keystone Fish Division, and when he left his Sassafras Street home, he was carrying a briefcase with $30,000. Weis had an appointment in Port Stanley, where he planned to purchase an Ontario fish processing business.

His plan for Keystone Fish was to emulate the business model of Captain William Kolbe, who owned commercial fish processing businesses in both Erie and Port Dover. The two-location, international Curtze operation would allow Keystone, like Kolbe Fish, to catch and process fish on the Canadian side of Lake Erie and then transport them to Erie to be sold into the lucrative U.S. market. Weis left for Conneaut, Ohio, where he barely made it to the *Marquette & Bessemer No. 2* in time for departure. Good luck, bad luck!

The *Marquette & Bessemer No. 2* was a 338-foot, steel railroad car-ferry designed to carry train cars filled with coal. It made regular round trips to Port Stanley, where it discharged coal cars from four sets of internal tracks and replaced them with empties. Occasionally, the *Marquette & Bessemer No. 2* also took coal to Port Dover, where it docked at the now underwater steel pier just west of today's municipal dock. In those days, car-ferries (both on Lake Erie and Lake Michigan) typically offered passenger service, providing cabins and food service.

Unfortunately for Albert Weis, a terrible late fall storm struck the car-ferry as it was crossing Lake Erie. A pitch-black sky, a wall of icy sleet and snow and winds of eighty miles per hour suddenly turned the lake into a frenzy. Hours after the overdue *Marquette & Bessemer No. 2* should have arrived at Port Stanley, observers saw it hesitate in front of the harbor entrance and then turn away. There was no way a ship could have entered Port Stanley that day, given the storm surge and waves inside the harbor. Days went by. Rumors began to circulate. An empty lifeboat washed up near the base of Long Point. Debris matching the ship's signature green and white colors began washing ashore between Port Burwell and Long Point. Some began to wonder if the *Marquette & Bessemer No. 2* had run aground near Long Point and if the crew might be stranded there. Erie newspaper headlines focused on Albert Weis and the missing briefcase filled with cash.

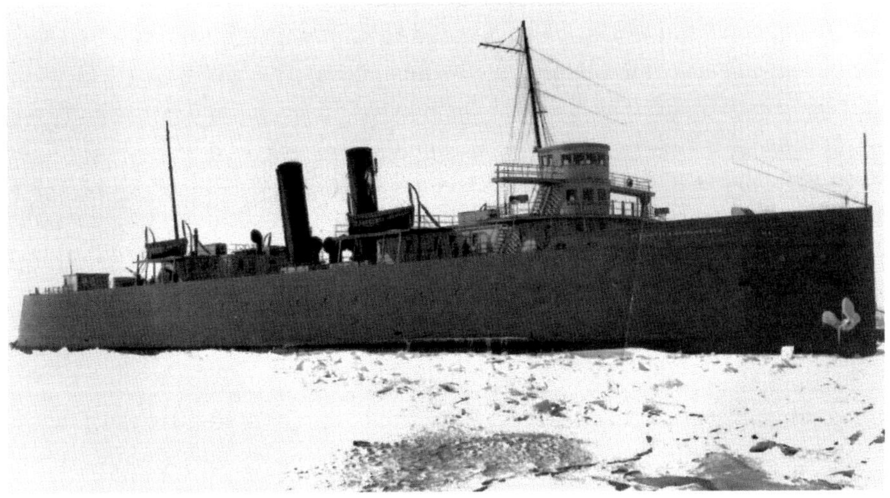

The *Marquette & Bessemer No. 2*. *Courtesy of Jerry Skrypzak.*

On Sunday morning, Captain Jeremy Driscol decided to take the Pennsylvania Fish Commission boat, *Commodore Perry*, across the lake to conduct a search of Long Point. As he left the dock, he told friends that he hoped to find Weis and the rest of the crew holed up somewhere on the wilderness peninsula or perhaps at the lighthouse keeper's home. The storm had severed communications with both the lighthouse and the lifesaving operations at the tip of the point.

Eight miles from the Erie Channel, Driscoll spotted a debris field punctuated by green- and white-colored wood. Slowly ducking between ice floes that had formed over the previous forty-eight hours, he followed the debris west, stopping to retrieve bits of wreckage. An hour into the trek, a crew member spotted a lifeboat floating inside the debris field. Driscoll headed toward it, and as he came closer, he noted that there were men sitting upright in the boat. The crew from the *Commodore Perry* waved and yelled, but there was no response. Upon reaching the stricken men, the reason became obvious. The men were dead. The upright sitting position of the crew was made possible only by the fact that that they were frozen solid in a cockpit-shaped block of ice that had formed around them.

Carefully tying lines to the overweighted lifeboat, Driscoll turned back toward Erie and began a painfully slow six-hour trip, taking care not to let the floating ice-coffin capsize. Unlike the *Marquette & Bessemer No. 2*, Driscoll had a ship-to-shore radio, which he used to alert authorities in Erie, and his radio message led to the huge crowd when he finally arrived.

The search for the *Marquette & Bessemer No. 2* has baffled wreck hunters. Confusing evidence caused by debris fields in two distinctly different locations, the recovery of several bodies the following spring in different places and the discovery of a third lifeboat outside Buffalo Harbor have added fuel to speculative fires. Where is the ship today? Why hasn't it been found? Has someone located it and kept the discovery a secret? Only time will tell.

PART IV
COMMERCIAL FISHING

Grace M (1904) and *Barnhurst* (1905): Lake Erie's Fish Wars

Captain Edward Dunn of the Canadian Revenue Service moved to Lake Erie with his newly armed research and patrol ship, *Petrel*. He soon learned, however, that his boat was not fast enough to catch many of the American fish tugs that were illegally setting nets near Long Point. Deciding that the Erie–Long Point corridor was ground zero in the fight against American fish piracy, Dunn lobbied for a newer and faster patrol boat, the *Vigilant*. Both the *Petrel* and the *Vigilant* spent most of their time in Port Dover, where Dunn could focus on Erie. During a press conference once, Dunn told the Canadian media that more than one hundred Erie tugs were regularly fishing in Ontario waters.

During the six-year period between 1900 and 1906, Dunn managed to seize thousands of illegal gill nets and capture more than twenty-five American fish tugs. The general practice in the early years was to allow captured American fishermen to sell their catch in Port Dover and use the proceeds to return to Erie, making the first arrests and seizures as much of a political game as serious business. Except for the shootings. The *Vigilant* was equipped with a bow-mounted Gatling gun. Knowing that American

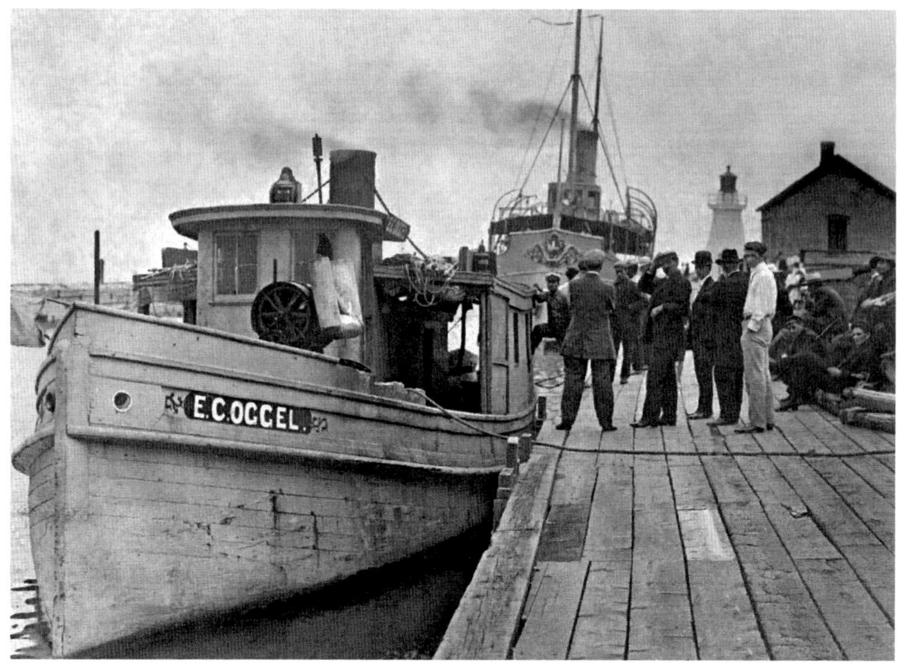

The *E.C. Oggel* from Erie and its crew, having been arrested at Port Dover with Captain Dunn tipping his hat. *Courtesy of Port Dover Harbour Museum.*

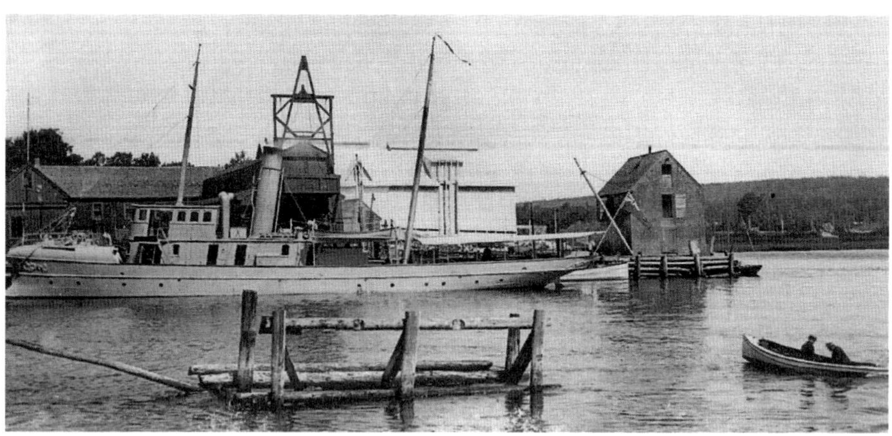

The Canadian revenue ship *Petrel* at Port Dover. *Courtesy of Jerry Skrypzak.*

fishermen who were fleeing from him would usually duck beneath the gunnels of their fish tugs, Dunn didn't hesitate to open fire on any tug that tried to escape. Usually these chases, in which Erie tugs often took advantage of head starts to outrun the *Vigilant*, resulted in escaped tugs with bullet hole–riddled topsides. The *Vigilant* was good for business in Erie. Larger, faster steam engines were often installed in fish tugs during winter seasons.

In November 1904, however, a chase turned out badly for both an American crew and for Dunn. In pursuit of the tug *Grace M*, Captain Dunn made a hard starboard turn to work his Gatling gun into a position to fire. Just as Dunn turned, however, the captain of the *Grace M*, which was on a parallel course on the *Vigilant*'s starboard side, made a sudden turn to port to evade capture. Seeing *Grace M* cross his bow, Dunn tried to reverse his maneuver, but it was too late. With a terrible grinding sound, the bow of the *Vigilant*, which was almost eight times as heavy as the *Grace M*, punctured and rolled the fish tug. Within minutes, the smaller fish tug had disappeared, propelled to the bottom by the impetus of the collision.

The sinking of the *Grace M* was the first of several signature events that shifted Lake Erie's fish wars from boyish frivolity to serious life-and-death business. Even though Dunn quickly slowed the *Vigilant* and came to the aid of its stricken crew, he was unable to save the tug, and two of the five-man crew were lost. The captain of the *Grace M* assumed responsibility for the incident, but media on both sides of Lake Erie suddenly lost their taste for Captain Dunn and his tactics. The *Grace M* affair also changed things for Erie's fishermen when the Canadian government reacted by shifting its laws dealing with captured American poachers. Beginning with the 1908 fishing season, American poachers were to be arrested and sent to prison rather than released to sell their fish and return to Erie.

The 1905 season was especially productive for Dunn and the *Vigilant*. With most of the "bugs" shaken out after an incomplete 1904 maiden season, Dunn had fine-tuned *Vigilant*'s steam engine and bragged to friends that the patrol ship could make speeds of fifteen miles per hour. In early September, Dunn also perfected a new technique for catching Erie tugs. He would anchor *Vigilant* behind Long Point and watch for an approaching boat. When he spotted a tug approaching, he would steam east toward Buffalo, creating the appearance that *Vigilant* was an ordinary freighter moving between Long Point and eastern Lake Erie. After a few miles, Dunn would swing around in a circle to the north while the fish tug tended its nets, cutting off the unsuspecting fishermen from escape to the south.

Between September 12 and 15, Dunn lured three Erie tugs into his trap. He captured the *E.C. Oggel* and the *Bertha Cockerell* and managed to riddle the *W.J. McCarter* with bullet holes. Captain Frank Hardy of the Keystone Fish Company's *McCarter* had been warned of Dunn's new tactics, and as soon as the crew spotted the *Vigilant* behind Long Point, they turned back and made a run for it. Dunn managed to pull within machine gun range of the *McCarter* before it could make it to the center of the lake and spray it with bullets, but the Erie tug escaped. Captain Tom Post of the Booth Company tug *Cockerell* was not so lucky. After several rounds from *Vigilant*'s machine gun shattered the wooden railing, he gave up and allowed himself to be towed to port. The *Cockrell* was impounded along with its equipment and six thousand pounds of fish. The *Oggel* suffered a similar fate when its captain, Burt Morrison, and the rest of his Keystone Fish Company crew were captured and towed to Port Dover. The tug and nets were impounded, but after a few days, the crew was allowed to return to Erie.

On Sunday, September 17, the Erie tug *Harry G Barnhurst* left its Booth Company docks to cross the lake. Captain Nick Fasel had set nets during the middle of the night two days earlier, a tactic that usually allowed Erie fish tugs to avoid detection. With the nets in the water for two days, there was a risk that the fish would be decaying. Fasel was aware of *Vigilant*'s stepped-up enforcement, but Booth Company agents in Port Dover had reported that Sunday was going to be a day off for the patrol ship.

At seventy-five feet in length, *Barnhurst* was oversized for a fish tug. It had originally been built as an excursion boat, and in addition to its size, it was said to be Erie's fastest tug. Captain Fasel and his crew of five—which included engineer Jerry Collin, fireman Magnus Johnson and deckhands Albert Hahan, Pat Owen and Frank Weschler—assumed that *Vigilant* would not be behind Long Point as they approached their nets four miles southwest of the tip of the point. Because the *Barnhurst* was so far west of the tip of Long Point, Fasel failed to notice the gray outline of the *Vigilant* as it slipped along behind the north beaches of the point and steamed away to the east. The crew worked quickly, rushing to pull the nets and get away. Their plan was to load the nets and then run for the safety of the mid-lake international line. Since the political reactions to the incident in which the *Vigilant* had chased the *Silver Spray* all the way across the lake, firing repeatedly until the tug had entered the channel, the captains of Erie's fish tugs knew that all they had to do to escape the clutches of the Canadians was to make it across the line.

Dunn had been publicly reprimanded for continuing an earlier chase into United States waters and firing his Gatling gun within hundreds of yards of Erie's channel. While the crew of the *Barnhurst* frantically dragged nets aboard and Captain Nick Fasel diligently watched for the *Vigilant* to appear from behind Long Point, the Canadian patrol vessel had already begun to circle behind them. Unbeknownst to Captain Fasel, Dunn had slipped into position between the Erie tug and the international line. Once Dunn was directly south of the *Barnhurst*, he stoked his boilers to full power and headed north. Engineer Jerry Collin spotted the *Vigilant* first, letting out a spontaneous yelp of alarm. The Canadian warship was bearing down on the *Barnhurst* at full speed, with clouds of black smoke indicating that its boilers were operating at maximum effort. With only moments to respond, Captain Fasel called his men to the wheelhouse and outlined a plan. Fireman Magnus Johnson was sent into the engine house, where his orders were to stoke the boilers "as if his life depended on it." Deckhand Frank Weschler, the most experienced crew member, joined Fasel in the wheelhouse to keep watch and help with navigation. The rest of the crew pretended not to see the *Vigilant* as they continued to retrieve nets. Nick Fasel was not about to give up his tug or his catch.

When the *Vigilant* was within firing range, Fasel yelled for the crew to lie flat on the decks. Even though the wooden gunnels offered minimal protection from the machine gun fire, he presumed that they would all be safest in the prone position. Meanwhile, Fasel was screaming for Magnus Johnson to stoke the boilers. Aboard *Vigilant*, Captain Dunn decided to cross *Barnhurt*'s stern and strafe its engine room. When he had closed to within fifty feet, Dunn ordered the gunner to fire. A loud staccato of bullets sprayed the *Barnhurst*. Several slugs ricocheted through the engine room, frightening Johnson, whose reaction was to stoke the boilers even harder. One bullet ripped through a wheelhouse wall, knocking a spoke out of the steering wheel. Fasel ducked and yelled for Frank Weschler to be ready to take over if he was hit. "Whatever you do, don't give up," Fasel barked, as Weschler watched the *Vigilant* pass across his stern.

Then Nick Fasel made the most daring maneuver of the day—a wild turn that inspired Captain Dunn to compliment the "crazy Erie fish tug captain" later. Fasel made a desperate hard turn to port, passing just behind *Vigilant*'s stern. Then he headed east on a new course, almost 180 degrees from the track that he had been following on his original escape route. At first, Dunn thought that the *Barnhurst* was surrendering and ordered *Vigilant* to slow. But Fasel careened through a tight turn, heeling the old fish tug more than twenty degrees. Then he steered downwind with the waves at his stern, heading almost directly for the U.S. border. Surfing on four- and five-foot

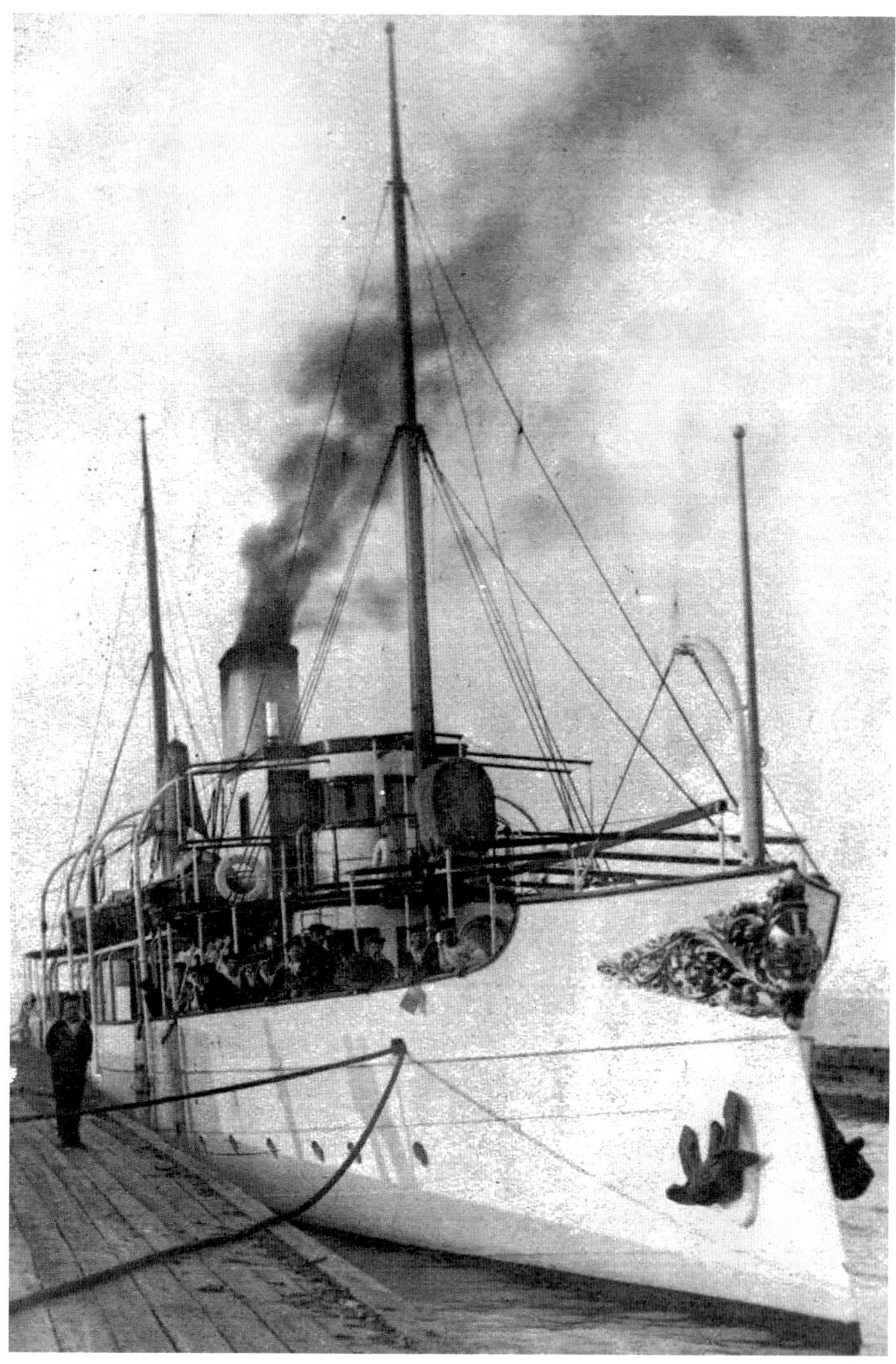

The Canadian revenue ship *Vigilant* at Port Dover. *Courtesy of Jerry Skrypzak.*

breakers, the *Barnhurst* suddenly had a speed advantage over *Vigilant*, which was too heavy to be helped along by the following seas.

The chase went on for another hour, and *Vigilant* fired several more times, but the *Barnhurst* slowly pulled out of range. By noon, the Erie fish tug was crossing the international line, and *Vigilant* was returning to Port Dover. Captain Fasel yelled to Johnson that he could let up on the boilers, and the old fish tug began to slow. It slowed and finally came to a full stop. Alarmed that Johnson had been hit by a bullet, Fasel and engineer Jerry Collin rushed to the engine room, where they found their friend lying motionless on the floor. They rolled him over to look for bullet wounds but found no signs of blood. Three hours later at the dock in Erie, a doctor revived Magnus Johnson and took him to Hamot Hospital, where it was determined that he had collapsed from the stress of the gunfight. Reporters counted more than fifty bullet holes in the *Barnhurst*, while Captain Fasel and his crew enjoyed newfound celebrity status. Headlines in the *Erie Dispatch* proclaimed Fasel and his crew "brave local heroes who had risked gunfire to bring whitefish and herring to town." Wooden tugs don't last forever, however, and the *Barnhurst* met its fate when it was destroyed by a fire that leveled the Keystone Fish Company.

Rocket (1910): Lake Erie's First Steel Fish Tug

During the spring of 1910, a brand-new Buffalo-built fish tug named *Rocket* was delivered to Erie's downtown docks for local fishermen Robert Tallman. At sixty-two feet in length and thirty-nine gross tons, the new tug was huge by conventional standards. There were a few larger fish tugs, but those were old-time excursion ships modified to serve the fishing business. The most amazing thing about the *Rocket*, however, was that it was Erie's first steel tug. Locals walked around the new tug inspecting its lines and kibitzing about the potential payload. The only other "iron ship" in Erie's harbor was the *Michigan*, and sadly, the old naval ship that had guarded Erie since the 1840s was so sluggish that it had become a bit of a joke. Fishermen who knocked on the *Rocket*'s gunnels wondered if this new steel tug would be the same—heavy, ponderous and slow.

After a few side-by-side runs to the fishing grounds with other tugs, however, it became obvious that *Rocket* was fast. It was overpowered, as

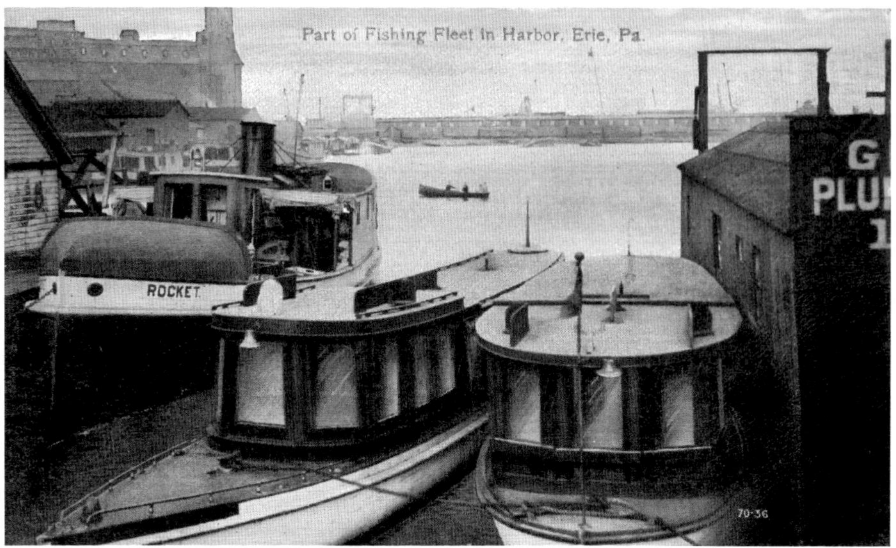

The *Rocket* at Erie's docks. *Courtesy of Jerry Skrypzak.*

anyone who crawled into the engine compartment learned, but *Rocket*'s speed was a result of its lines. It had a high bow and a tall sheer that made it slide effortlessly through waves, and its lines dropped gracefully to just a few feet of freeboard at the stern. *Rocket* was elegant as well as fast, and when fully loaded, it didn't settle into the water like the older wooden tugs. Its displacement and seven-foot draft also made it especially sea-kindly. Perhaps its greatest attribute, however, was that the steel hull acted as a bulletproof vest when *Rocket* crossed the international line to fish. *Rocket*'s first few years of service coincided with the early days of Lake Erie's fish wars, and as Captain Dunn once said, his Canadian patrol ship didn't have a fighting chance against the new armor-plated fish tug from Erie. Captain Talliman and his crew would regularly take their steel tug into Canadian waters to fish, and when *Petrel* approached, they would continue pulling nets until it came within firing range and then speed away with the crew ducking for cover behind the steel gunnels.

It was the taunting of the *Rocket* and its crew that inspired Dunn to argue for a faster, better-armed patrol ship. Dunn complained to superiors that within a few years, all of Erie's fish tugs would be as fast as the *Rocket* and steel plated, and he would have no chance of protecting "Canadian" fish. In effect, the *Rocket* helped Dunn to rationalize a newer, faster and better-armed patrol boat. When Dunn launched the *Vigilant* in 1904, *Rocket* stopped fishing the

Canadian side of the lake and began making trips to the western end instead. Talliman knew about the improved armaments on the *Vigilant* and realized that he would be a marked man if Dunn ever saw him fishing in Canadian waters again. Instead of tempting fate, he changed fishing grounds.

It was on one of those western runs from Erie in 1905 that *Rocket* had an unfortunate accident. Unlike the welded steel tugs that were to appear later, *Rocket* was a composite boat, made of metal plate fastened to a wooden frame, and like most prototypes, it was not without problems. The combination of its heavy displacement, overpowered engine and speed put such a strain on the hull joinery that by its second year, it was beginning to leak badly. On April 13, 1905, while crashing through heavy waves with a load of fish, *Rocket* started to take on so much water that the pumps couldn't keep up. The captain made an emergency run for shore just east of Cleveland, but he didn't quite make it, and *Rocket* sank on a sandbar in twenty feet of water just a few feet from the breakwall. Fortunately, the crew managed to scramble safely to shore.

Rocket was raised, rebuilt and continued to fish until 1918, but the skeptics who had argued that its steel hull would not stand the test of time seemed vindicated, and the wholesale technical shift to steel fish tugs did not follow as quickly as it might have if *Rocket* had not had structural problems. By the 1920s, the Gamble Yard in Port Dover was beginning to produce lighter, faster and more reliable welded steel tugs, and *Rocket* seemed like a failed experiment. A Detroit sand and gravel company purchased *Rocket* and converted it to a work tug for hauling barges of aggregate.

In 1930, after welded construction evolved, builders began to use steel instead of wooden frames, which made the second generation of welded tugs stronger and lighter. Ultimately, the *Rocket* was rebuilt from the inside out with a metal frame, but it was still heavy and ponderous compared to the newer all-welded tugs. In 1941, it was moved to Port Arthur, Ontario, where it continued as a work tug until 1969.

The Fish Tug *Peerless* (1924): Problems with Gasoline

The 1920s were troubling times for commercial fishermen. "Old-timers" were clinging to steam engines and boilers, a technology that had served

Ceaseless Search of Lake Fails To Produce Trace of Missing Erie Men Who Lost Their Lives As Tug Burned

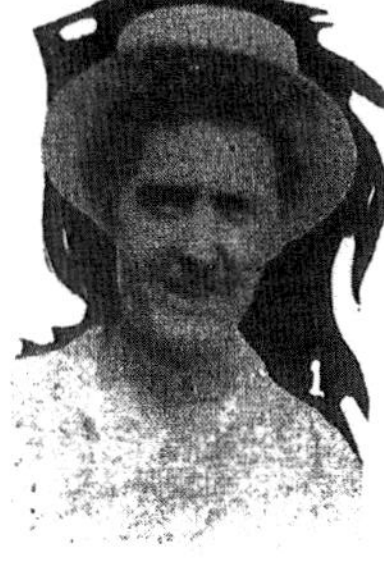

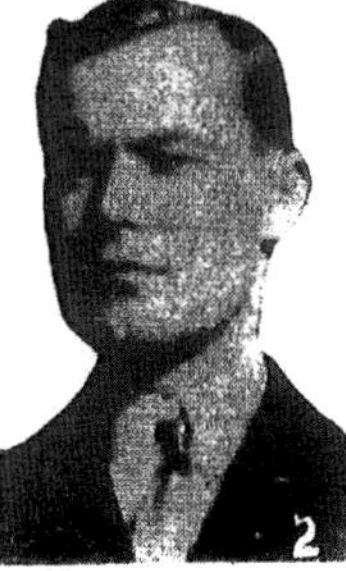

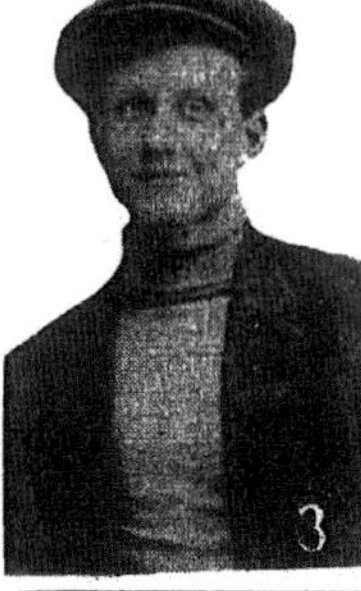

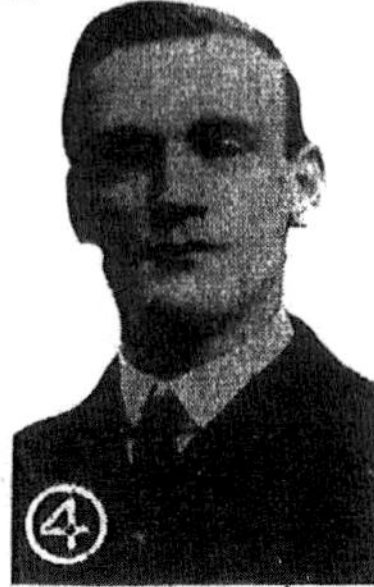

(By a Staff Correspondent.)

Wireless from aboard S. S. Islander, off Peele Island, April 27.—Lake Erie still holds her dead. After 30 hours of terrible but ever hopeful watching this boat, with two others, has set back for the home port—Sandusky, Ohio.

The Peerless of Erie is gone. With her, Captain Andrew Forbeck and three of his crew. Two others, Michael Tansey and Edward Rindfuss, who were close together in life, were found floating together, lifeless, early Saturday morning.

It is a tragic story. A square-sterned fishing tug with a leaky gasoline pipe. Engine trouble. Then an explosion, and death by fire or water.

Against a background of night the burning Peerless presented a weird figure. A passing steamer, attracted by the dying blaze, came close by in hope of picking up survivors. But there was none. Three miles away the rigid bodies of Rindfuss and Tansey, encircled by life-preservers were taken aboard.

With Captain Forbeck and three of his crew missing the cry for succor sounded along the entire length of Lake Erie.

At dawn Sunday morning the Islander, commanded by Captain C. F. Mischler, president of the United Fisheries Co., of Sandusky, set out of port. Two smaller boats accompanied the Islander.

Heading almost due north we crossed Lake Erie to a point within a half mile of where the floating bulk of the smoldering Peerless was last seen by the Otto Reiss.

(Continued on page 2, column 1.)

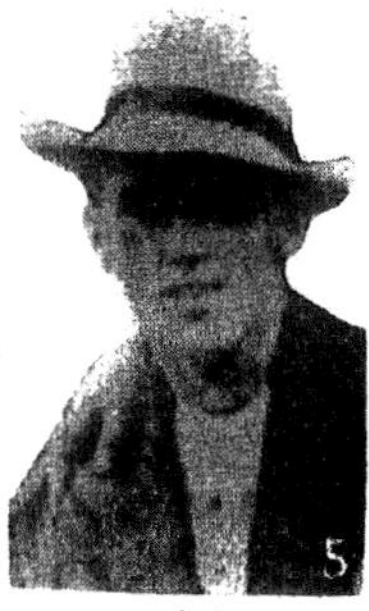

'TOO GAME TO QUIT' TANSEY GOES TO A DEATH HE FEARED

Meets End With Dear Pal Who Was the Best Man at His Wedding.

Michael Tansey went to his death with the other members of the crew of the fish tug Peerless because he was "too game to quit." He foretold the disaster that impended and yet, though it was on the very eve of his wedding anniversary and an affectionate kiss was on the lips of the wife who had been his faithful helpmate for eight years, he went aboard the craft and so to his doom.

Mrs. Tansey had been in Sandusky with her husband while the Peerless was fishing out of that port. When orders came to the crew to quit that port on Friday morning, lift their nets and put into Fairport, she prepared to return to Erie by train. This was on Thursday evening and the Peerless was due to clear from Sandusky at 3 a. m.

"I am afraid the boat will blow up and send us all to the bottom," said Tansey as he gathered his wife in his arms for what was to prove their final farewell. "There's something radically wrong with her engine most of the time."

(Continued on page 2, column 3.)

MISSING CREW.

The Times has made arrangements with every port along Lake Erie to telegraph immediate word concerning discovery of the bodies of any of the four missing members of the tug Peerless.

Officials of the Keystone Fish Co. are in constant touch with Sandusky, Vermillion, O., and other points along the lake shore, nearly abreast the place where the Peerless was last seen.

All hope has been abandoned for the safety of four members of the crew.

Missing members of the Peerless crew are:

Captain Forbeck, 147 East Seventh street.

Leo Boyd, engineer, 215 Chestnut street.

William Pfister, 514 West Third street.

Adolphe Rohman, 212 Cherry street.

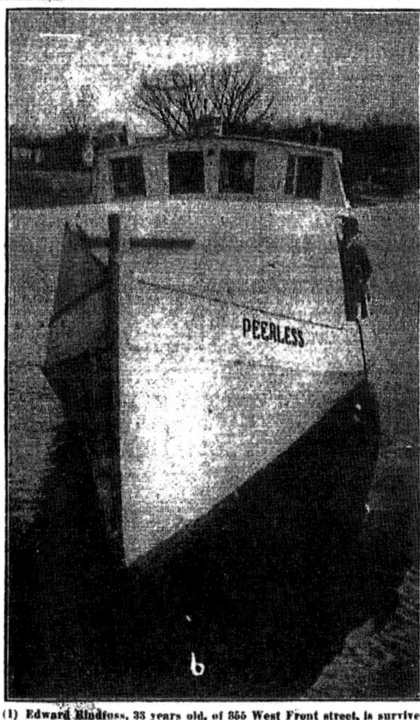

(1) Edward Rindfuss, 33 years old, of 355 West Front street, is survived by his mother, Mary Rindfuss. There are also three sisters, Mrs. Mary Michaels, of 257 West Third street; Mrs. Nellie O'Hearn, of Short street, and Mrs. Brundage, of Los Angeles, Cal., and one brother, George Rindfuss. Funeral services will be held at 9 o'clock Wednesday morning in St. Patrick's church.

(2) Leo Boyd, engineer, 38 years old, of 215 Chestnut street, is survived by his wife, Walburga Boyd, and two children, Elaine, 6, and Thomas, 5. Also two brothers, Thomas J. Boyd, of 3105 Plum street, and Hubert Boyd, of 1114 West Sixth street, and three sisters, Mrs. George W. Dailey, 440 West Second street; Mrs. Joseph Sitterle, of 362 West Fourth street, and Mrs. F. A. Healy, of 2917 Cherry street. Body not recovered.

(3) William Pfister, 33 years old, of 514 West Third street, is survived by his wife, Marie, and two children, Helen, 13, and William, Jr., 7. Also his father and mother of 543 West Third street, and sisters, Mrs. A. J. Louch, of 719 West Fifth street; Helen Pfister, 543 West Third street; brothers, Neal Pfister, of 224 Walnut street, and Lawrence Pfister, of 545 West Third street. Body has not been recovered.

(4) Michael Tansey, 41 years old, of 407 West Third street, is survived by his wife, Clara Karch Tansey, and his father and mother. Also one

Peerless newspaper headlines from Erie. *Courtesy of Jerry Skrypzak.*

Great Lakes vessels for almost a century. "Modern" fishermen were making a transition from steam to gasoline and advocating the reduction of a crew member (the fireman). Smaller crews resulted in more money to go around when there was a good catch. But veteran fishermen shook their heads in grim silence at the suggestion of gasoline engines, arguing that such contraptions had no place on the water. A tiny gasoline leak, almost inevitable on a small working boat, could quickly turn a tug into a bomb. There was a second argument in favor of steam engines, however, one that seemed connected to whitefish. Old-timers noted that the demise of whitefish coincided precisely with the advent of gasoline-powered fish tugs. While it was (and still is) difficult to draw scientific linkages between these events, there was no arguing with steam and boiler men. "Something about burning coal on the water was natural," they said. "Either the coal dust, the smoke or the clinkers that were regularly tossed overboard must have been good for the whitefish."

On Friday morning, April 25, 1924, the Erie fish tug *Peerless*, working for Keystone Fish Company, left Sandusky to tend nets set in the western end of the lake near the Islands. Like many fishermen, Captain Andy Forbeck and his crew had been spending the early spring upstream of the ice floes that had been keeping Lake Erie's Central and Eastern Basin fishermen in port. The ice was beginning to break up, however, and Forbeck told friends in Sandusky that he was going to pull his nets, pick and pack the whitefish and herring and then head for Erie. When the weather turned sour that morning, with winds increasing to forty miles per hour, most of the Sandusky fish tugs limped back into port, leaving their gill nets untended. Had it not been for the expectation that *Peerless* was heading back to Erie later that day, and that following winds and seas would have been pushing it east, Captain Forbeck's Ohio friends would have been more concerned by late afternoon when everyone else was safely back at the Sandusky tug harbor.

At suppertime, reports of a massive ball of flames sighted off Pelee Island, directly offshore from Sandusky, had begun to reach the community. There was a persistent rumor that a fish tug had burned north of Sandusky in the gill netting grounds. The reports were reinforced by episodic radio transmissions from Lake Erie bulk ships transiting the Pelee Passage, north of the gill netting grounds. In Erie, Keystone Fish officials heard the radio reports and began to worry about their missing tug. At first, there was hope that the *Peerless* and its crew had put into Cleveland or Ashtabula to wait out the storm. Erie papers responded with a Saturday headline about Captain Forbeck and the crew of the *Peerless* being missing.

On Saturday afternoon, a telephone communication from Pelee Island reached Sandusky to confirm that a fish tug that was burned to the waterline had washed up on a beach carrying two bodies. The victims, who were discovered on the burnt hull, seemed to have died from exposure rather than burns. By the time this message reached the Erie offices of Keystone Fish, a report from the eastbound steamer *Otto M Reis* noted that its crew had spotted two fish tugs that had burned to the waterline, one near Pelee, Ohio, and another north of the Pennsylvania–New York state line. The incomplete report from the *Reis*, which did not have a ship-to-shore radio, added that the bodies of the two fish tug crew members had been recovered and that they were bringing them to Buffalo. When Keystone officials arrived in Buffalo to identify the bodies, they were disappointed to learn that the *Otto M Reis* had not been able to get close enough to the *Peerless* to recover its crew. Instead, they had retrieved the bodies from the other burned tug, which turned out to be the *Grace* from Dunkirk, New York.

An official investigation managed to make sense of the confusing reports. The conclusion was that the crew of *Peerless*, anxious to recover the gill nets and return to Erie, had continued pulling nets in a rising storm near some of Lake Erie's most turbulent waters. The shallows between Sandusky and the Islands, while productive early spring gill netting grounds, have always been prone to sudden wave changes because of prevailing southwesterly winds, currents that are channeled between the Islands and shoaling waters. Bouncing up and down as they were retrieving their nets, a fuel line probably began to leak, after which a spark ignited the wooden tug. It was suspected that the crew of the *Peerless* went into the water to avoid the flames and hung on to the side waiting for the fire to subside. Apparently, only two crew members were able to climb back aboard, where they ultimately died of exposure in the ice-cold winds, rain and sleet that pummeled Lake Erie for more than twenty-four hours. It was noted that the *Peerless* and the *Grace* were both wooden-hulled, gasoline-powered fish tugs and that until fish tug crews became more skillful at handling the volatile fuel, there were likely to be more such tragedies.

THE STEAMER *LOUISE* (1931): LAKE ERIE'S LAST COMMERCIAL FISH TRANSPORT SHIP

It's mid-December in Erie, perfect shipwreck-hunting weather. Securing my PFD (I have only mastered the first half of the Eskimo roll), I launch my trusty sixteen-foot kayak from the Erie Yacht Club and paddle east. It is a crisp winter day, and the wind has been calm for a week. The water is as clear as an aquarium. The exceptional clarity reveals bottom features at more than six feet as rocks and freshwater mussel shells pass underneath the kayak. Erie sailmaker Dave Bierig brought the underwater location of the old steamship *Louise* to my attention. A year ago, we had been sitting in his sailmaking loft on Presque Isle Bay when he told me that low water levels had brought the steamer *Louise* almost to the surface. Then he shared several stories about hapless power boaters who had lost propellers by colliding with the *Louise*'s nearly intact boiler.

The *Louise* has an interesting Port Dover/Erie connection. The boat was originally built in Sandusky, Ohio, by John Monk, who also designed its sister ship, the *City of Dresden*, the famous "whiskey ship" that foundered off Long Point in 1922, spilling a load of Prohibition-era booze. Both the *Louise* and *City of Dresden* served in a variety of duties over their long lives. They were package freighters and excursion ships, but during the heyday of commercial fishing, they served as bulk fish transport ships. The *City of Dresden* worked the Port Stanley–Cleveland route, while the *Louise*, which was owned by local (both Erie and Port Dover) innovator William "Cap" Kolbe, hauled fish between Port Dover and Erie.

During Lake Erie's peak whitefish and herring days, when Port Dover fishermen caught more than the Ontario market could absorb, Kolbe sent his son, Robert, off to college to invent flash freezing, which he did as a junior engineering student at Rensselaer in upstate New York. Once the process was perfected, William Kolbe would flash-freeze fish in his Port Dover plant and ship them in bulk to Erie using the *Louise*. Since Erie was connected by rail to New York and Chicago, Kolbe was able to fetch a better price for his Port Dover catch by moving frozen fish to Erie and then loading them onto railroad cars for transport to Chicago and New York.

Changes in the fishing business spelled the end of the useful life of the *Louise*. Kolbe switched to the use of faster, more fuel-efficient fish tugs for runs to Erie; railroad lines reached Port Dover, opening the Toronto and London markets; and finally, the whitefish and herring catches declined.

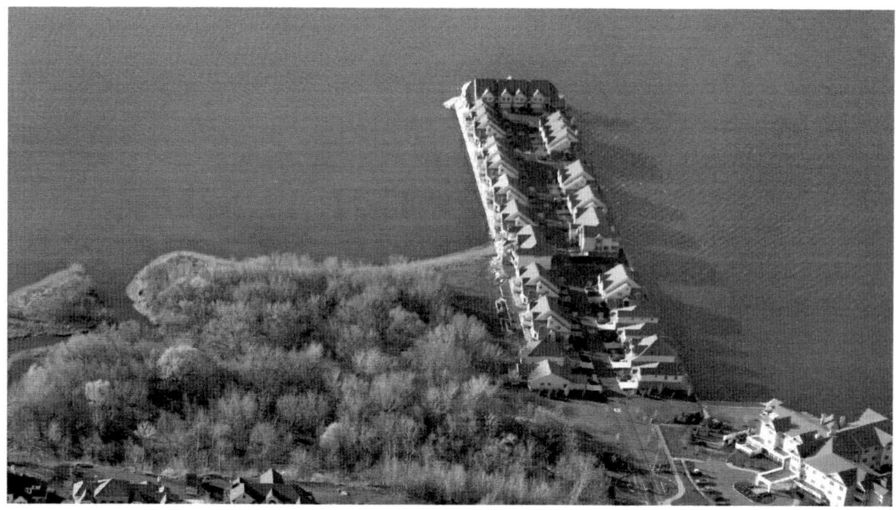

The steamer *Louise* lies on the bottom just west (left) of the Cascade Docks, which now house upscale condominiums. *Courtesy of Jerry Skrypzak.*

Suddenly, there was no use for an aging eighty-seven-foot wooden ship. *Louise* was too be big to be a fish tug and too small for a package freighter.

The *Louise* languished in several Canadian ports until 1930, when an Erie businessman purchased it and moved the fifty-two-year-old veteran to the East Slip while he decided what to do with it. The stately old lady (renamed *Hunter Willis*) was tethered to a dock in the midst of Erie's commercial fishing fleet, which was primarily populated by smaller, steel-hulled tugs. Neighboring fishermen complained that it was taking up space that would have been better served being filled by a modern fish tug.

On the evening of October 22, 1931, a plume of black smoke was seen rising from the *Louise/Hunter Willis*. An investigation revealed a below-deck fire. In an effort to keep the flames from spreading, a posse of fishermen untied *Louise*, and within minutes, the old ship was being towed into the bay by a fish tug filled with volunteer helpers. The good Samaritans hatched a plan to tow *Louise* to the west end of Presque Isle Bay and sink it in Erie's traditional scuttling grounds, where a number of old wooden ships were lying just below the surface near the head of Presque Isle Bay. The fishermen who were towing the *Louise* assumed that they would be able to save its structure and machinery by sinking it in shallow water, where its owners could salvage it later. They were also doing their fellow East Slip residents a favor by removing a potential harbor torch that could have done significant damage to the other boats, as well as the docks and buildings where it was berthed.

As they approached the Cascade Docks (west of the Public Dock), however, it was becoming obvious that the breeze that was being fanned by the speed of the tow was accelerating the flames. When they passed the dock, a wall of fire rose from the wheelhouse, and a cloud of black smoke stretched for almost half a mile behind them. Slowing the speed of the tow to dampen the flames, they ducked behind (south of) the Cascade Dock and scuttled the *Louise* in twelve feet of water. Even though much of the ship's topsides and hull remained intact, and though the boiler and engine seemed unharmed, an inspection a few days later convinced the owner to abandon it. Within a few years, the ravages of winter ice had ground down most of its topsides, and by the post–World War II era, the *Louise* had become one more of Erie's forgotten derelicts—a fleet of old schooners, wooden fish tugs and canal packets that had been towed to out-of-the-way places in Presque Isle Bay and sunk.

Sixty-nine years and two months later, my yellow kayak came to a stop a few feet above the remains of the *Louise*. Its gunnels, although buried in sand, were largely intact, and many of its ribs were clearly visible. The boiler stood almost vertically, rising to within a few feet of the water's surface. I reached down and touched the boiler with the tip of a paddle, noting scars that represented propellers that had been destroyed during low-water years. Suspended over the *Louise* in a magical moment of contemplation, I asked myself for the thousandth time why I was so smitten with memories of old ships and their sailors. I remembered William Kolbe, Port Dover, ships and shipwrecks that I have come to know over the years.

PART V
NEW BUSINESS MODELS

The Daring Young Man in a Flying Machine (1912): Shipwrecks Were Not Just for Ships

On February 20, 1912, headlines from New York to Chicago heralded a historic event: "North America's First International Air Flight," an adventure that linked Erie, Pennsylvania, with Long Point, Ontario. Erie adventurer and daredevil Earl "Birdman" Sandt taxied down the frozen surface of Presque Isle Bay, circled over the Public Dock, wagged his "aeroplane" wings and disappeared into the northern sky and destiny. Erie's daredevil aviator had declared his intention to cross Lake Erie, land at Long Point and return in just a few hours, so the crowd milled about the bayfront, waiting. Hours passed, darkness set in and people began to wander away.

"Told him it couldn't be done," muttered an old-time fisherman who had shared his knowledge of Long Point. "We'll find his body floating in the spring," he added. It would be almost midnight before Earl Sandt finally made his way back to Erie—without his aeroplane. But he did ultimately return to tell his story, become one of the city's favorite sons and make his mark as a pioneer American aviator.

Lewis Earl Sandt was born in Brookville, Pennsylvania, in 1888. His father was a well-to-do pharmacist who hoped to convince his son to follow

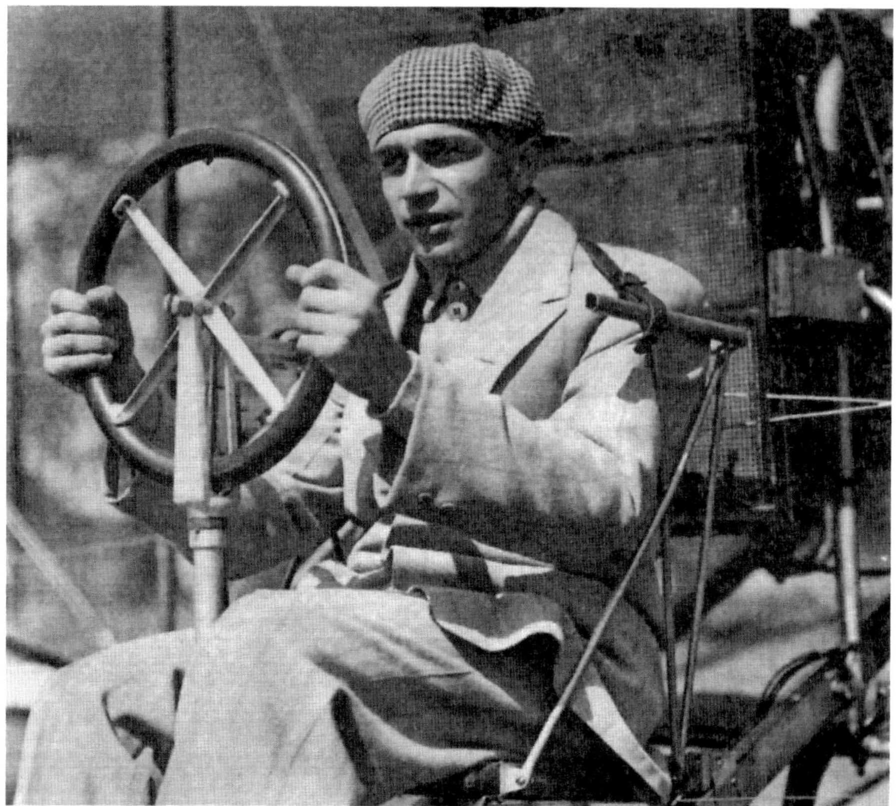

Earl "Birdman" Sandt in the seat of his Curtiss biplane. *Courtesy of Erie County Historical Society.*

in his footsteps. But Earl had other ideas. He was fascinated by mechanical things, and his love of gasoline engines led him to become a mechanic. He was the first person in Brookville to drive a motorcycle and then an automobile. In 1908, he and his brother moved to Erie, where they opened a downtown garage specializing in automobile and motorcycle repair.

Stories of the Wright brothers and early aviation fascinated Earl, and he became obsessed with flying. When Earl worked for his father as a young man, he saved his salary and managed to build an impressive bank account. Using savings as well as money that he earned at Sandt Brothers Garage, he traveled to New York State and enrolled in a three-week flight course offered by the Curtiss Aircraft Company. With encouragement from Glen Curtiss, Earl purchased a small plane shortly after graduation from flight school. It was a biplane with a sixty-horsepower, rear-mounted engine. The pilot sat forward in a lightweight rattan chair, from which he operated the rudder with a circular steering wheel. Earl hid his obsession from his father, even though he was planning to use his flying machine to earn money.

His first flight along Erie's lakeshore in November 1911 ended in near disaster when he crash-landed. Later, he began taking friends for short flights and hauling the plane to county fairs to earn money. After a few months of barnstorming, Sandt realized that he needed a major event to propel him toward fame and fortune. By the time of his planned flight across Lake Erie, Earl's father had learned of his son's intentions and publicly proclaimed his son to be a young fool.

The choice of February for the fight was actually a clever promotional idea. Earl knew that a huge crowd would watch him take off from the frozen bay near the downtown docks and that the publicity would be invaluable when spring flying season arrived later that year. He was also careful to research his plan, taking time to chat with commercial fisherman who knew the lake and Long Point. Local papers were filled with news of the event, and on a cold, crisp Saturday afternoon at 2:30 p.m., Earl towed his biplane onto the ice opposite Erie's brand-new Public Dock and fired up the engine. The crowd cheered wildly as the plane lifted off the ice, and Sandt climbed slowly skyward into a moderate northwesterly breeze and disappeared over Presque Isle, swinging his tiny aircraft into a position that was approximately beam to wind.

Sandt sat in the rattan seat in front of the wings, where he was exposed to the bitterly cold wind as he headed north. True to Lake Erie's cantankerous nature, the farther he flew and the higher he rose, while attempting to spot the tip of Long Point, the harder the wind blew. By the time he had covered half the distance, Sandt could see that he was crabbing terribly to the east. When he finally spotted Long Point, he was well east of it, but he took a visual bearing on the lighthouse and turned upwind, hoping to find a landing spot on the ice south of the beaches.

Winter conditions had been harsh, and the ice on the south side of Long Point was crowned by pressure ridges. By the time Sandt decided that there was no way he could land on the south side of Long Point, he knew that he would not have enough fuel to make it back to Erie. His plan, in the case of running low on fuel, had been to ask the lighthouse keeper for gasoline. Commercial fisherman had advised him that there would almost always be a keeper at the light on weekends preparing for the opening of spring shipping season.

Determined to land, Sandt flew over the lighthouse, startling keeper William Porritt, and continued along the northern beaches toward Pottahawk

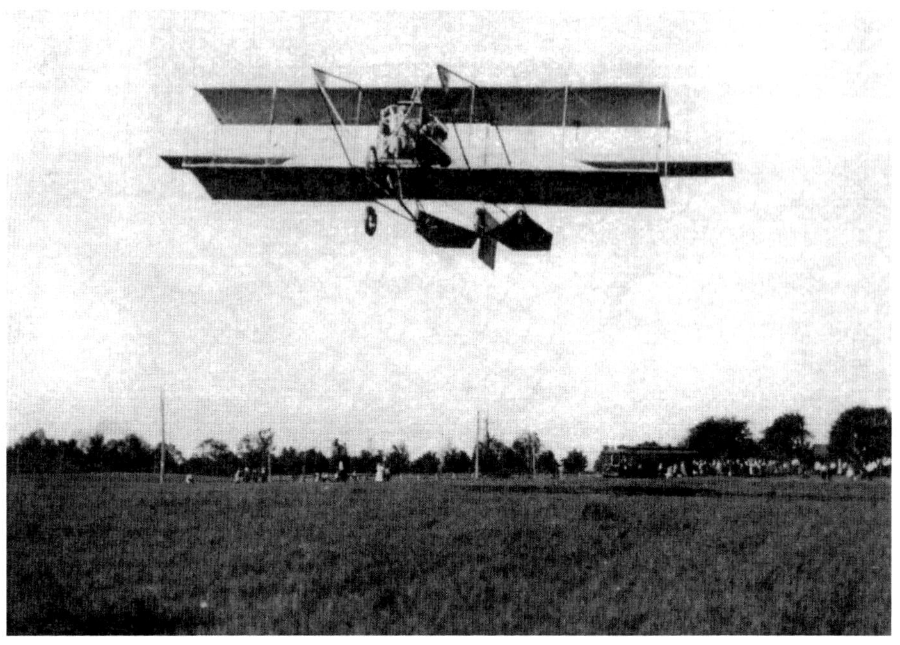

Sandt's biplane taking off. *Courtesy of Erie County Historical Society.*

Point. But he was running out of fuel, so he circled and returned to the tip of the point, this time searching for smooth ice north of the lighthouse. Passing over the lighthouse for a final time, he was thrilled to see a promising spot a few hundred feet from the beaches, where he brought his aeroplane down at 3:25 p.m. Sandt introduced himself to the lighthouse keeper, who offered to find some fuel. By this time, Earl realized that he was at risk of not making it back to Erie in time to capitalize on the crowd that had sent him off and the publicity that he was seeking. But he hurried, and within a few hours, several containers of gasoline had been liberated from the lighthouse keeper's boathouse and dragged across the ice to the plane. At 5:50 p.m., a grateful Earl Sandt waved goodbye to his new friend, taxied across the ice and disappeared to the south. This time, the cold winds that had slowed Sandt on his northerly trip lifted and pushed him, and with darkness closing in, Earl spotted the lights of Erie and began a long slow bank to the west hoping to drop onto the bay ice just inside the channel.

All seemed to be going well until Sandt was four miles from the channel and the engine began to sputter. There was plenty of gasoline in the tank, but the old fuel that had been transferred from the lighthouse keeper's boathouse contained destabilizing impurities. Sandt tried everything that he could to keep the engine running, but he was soon gliding engineless only a few feet above the frozen lake. Realizing that he would never make Erie's harbor, Sandt swung his plane to the east and frantically looked for a smooth spot on the ice. Just before darkness, he picked an opening between two pressure ridges and made a rough landing about four miles off North East's Freeport Beach. The landing went smoothly until the front wheel struck an ice outcropping, the plane buckled and Sandt was thrown fifty feet forward, landing unconscious on the ice.

By the time Earl Sandt came to his senses, several hours had passed, it was pitch black and he was bruised and shivering violently. Before Sandt hurried to shore to find shelter, he pushed the damaged plane into an opening between two ice ridges and did his best to secure it with an ice anchor. Then he hurried across the ice toward the lights of North East. By the time he reached shore, he was shivering uncontrollably and near exhaustion. Knocking repeatedly on doors, he finally found a friendly person who warmed him up and fed him. Then he made his way to the North East/Erie streetcar terminal and caught the 11:00 p.m. trolley back to Erie. He had been torn between returning to the ice with volunteers from North East to rescue his crippled plane and traveling to Erie to cash in on the publicity that his trip could offer. Finally, the darkness and cold convinced him to leave for Erie and report his adventures to the newspapers.

Late the next day, Sandt returned to retrieve his airplane. His plan was to remove the wings and tow it to shore, where it could be repaired. When Sandt and his friends got to the lakeshore, however, much had changed. The wind had shifted to the south, and a wide strip of open water had appeared. Features that Earl recalled from his desperate evening trek across the frozen tundra just the evening before had disappeared. Sandt searched for the plane but never found it. It almost certainly sank through the ice, where it now represents an unusual and uncharted Lake Erie Quadrangle disaster. Someday a lucky diver might stumble on it and wonder how an antique airplane could have found its way to the bottom of Lake Erie.

Undaunted, "Birdman" Sandt raised $500 with a newspaper plea, added some of his own money and recruited backers who were willing to help pay for his next airplane. The next spring, Sandt took up stunt flying in earnest, traveling with his brother and two other mechanics (he called them his "magicanics") to carnivals and fairs throughout Pennsylvania and Ohio, where he performed amazing feats of daring. Dives, loops and other maneuvers made Sandt a crowd favorite. He performed in Pittsburgh, flying over three rivers; traveled to Ohio, where he became the first pilot to carry airmail; and began taking paid passengers in a tandem seat.

Earl Sandt died in 1916 following a barnstorming accident at the Grove City, Pennsylvania summer fair. He had planned to take off from the fairgrounds, climb to an astounding 3,500 feet and thrill the crowd with a series of power dives and acrobatic maneuvers. Somehow his airplane was caught in an updraft shortly after takeoff, however, and it spun out of control. As the plane rolled and then plunged toward the ground, Sandt extracted himself from the seat and jumped (without a parachute) from an altitude of 1,000 feet.

The crowd held its collective breath as the daring young man turned and twisted his body like a high diver, frantically trying to point his feet toward the ground. He almost straightened himself up perfectly but landed in a strained position on one leg. Sinking to his hips in the mud of a soft field, he seemed to be all right at first. But his leg was so badly broken that he had to be carried away in a stretcher. Doctors did the best they could to straighten his leg, but Sandt grew sicker by the day. Finally, physicians recognized the symptoms of lockjaw (tetanus) and sent to Erie for a vaccine. Sadly, the medicine arrived one day too late, and Earl Sandt passed away on June 22, 1916. Some years later, in 1930, Charles Lindbergh's mother traveled to the site of Earl Sandt's grave to honor the pioneering aviator with a wreath. "Here lies one of the most important heroes in the history of flying," she whispered to a crowd of admirers.

There are several other airplane wrecks lying at the bottom of Lake Erie. While Earl Sandt's Curtist biplane (or what may be left of it) awaits discovery, side-scanning has revealed an intact World War II–era Lancaster west of Long Point, as well as a military DC-3 close to the tip of the point.

Colonial (1925): Lake Erie's Excursion Business

Between the late 1800s and the post–World War II era, when automobiles became common, Lake Erie entrepreneurs developed specialty excursion ships. Unlike the earlier upper-cabin steamships like the *Erie* and the *Atlantic*, the new excursion ships were developed to serve special vacation destinations—a network of grand hotels and other holiday destinations that was largely inaccessible except by the water. Excursion ships did not feature overnight

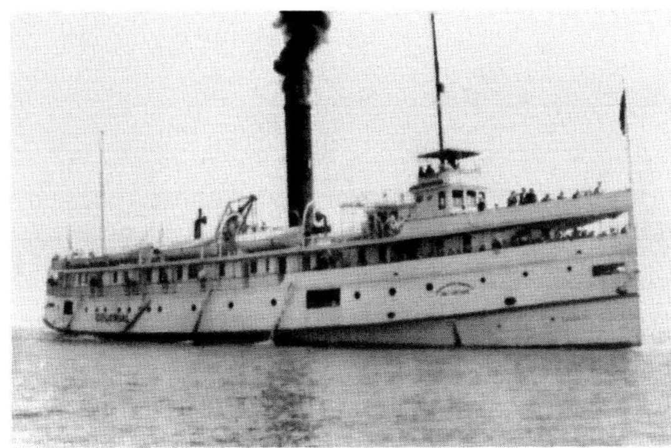

The *Colonial. Courtesy of Jerry Skrypzak.*

sleeping accommodations, and the lack of cabins allowed them to carry huge crowds on relatively short trips to destinations like Niagara Falls (Buffalo), Put-in-Bay, Detroit's Bobablo Island, Crystal Beach, Port Dover and Erie. Erie's local excursion destination was at the "head" on the western end of Presque Isle Bay, where there was a series of grand Victorian hotels.

For several years, Erie's homeport excursion ship was the *Colonial*, a 238-foot, steel-hulled propeller ship. *Colonial* was launched in 1885 and designed for the passenger business, but it was put into service too late for that business and proved to be a failure. In 1921, it was reworked as a specialty excursion ship and brought to Erie, where it became a fixture at the Public Dock with its gleaming white paint and polished brightwork. The *Colonial* quickly became a local favorite and source of community pride. In addition to its excursion runs, it provided corporate outings, moonlight cruises and regular weekly ferry service to Port Dover.

On August 11, 1925, *Colonial* disembarked eight hundred moonlight cruise passengers and immediately departed for Dunkirk, New York, to pick up an excursion group headed for Crystal Beach, Ontario, the next morning. Shortly after clearing the channel, Captain Parsons retired for the evening and handed over the helm to the first mate, who continued to steam east through calm seas. At 1:30 a.m., however, the crew spotted smoke coming from the bow. Upon investigating, the men found a raging fire that had ignited a locker filled with the ship's life preservers.

When the agitated crew reported the fire, First Mate David Robinson turned the helm to starboard (toward land) and sounded the whistle to alert the fire crew. Unfortunately, the ship's engineer misinterpreted the whistle and shut the engines down. Without the engines, the emergency crew could not operate the emergency fire hoses, and within a few minutes of the discovery of the fire, the *Colonial* was dead in the water and doomed.

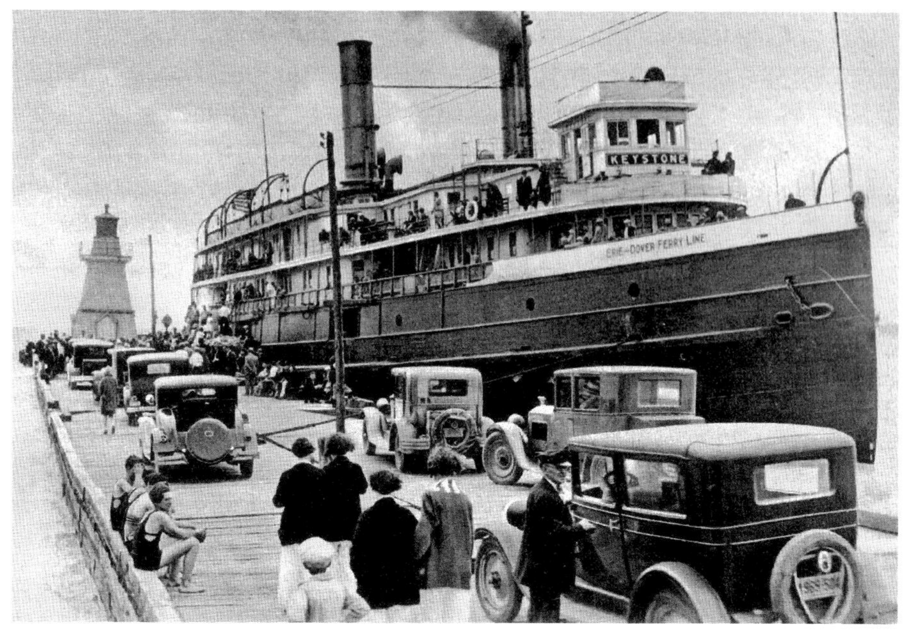

The *Keystone*, one of Nicholson's ferries, at Port Dover. *Courtesy of Jerry Skrypzak.*

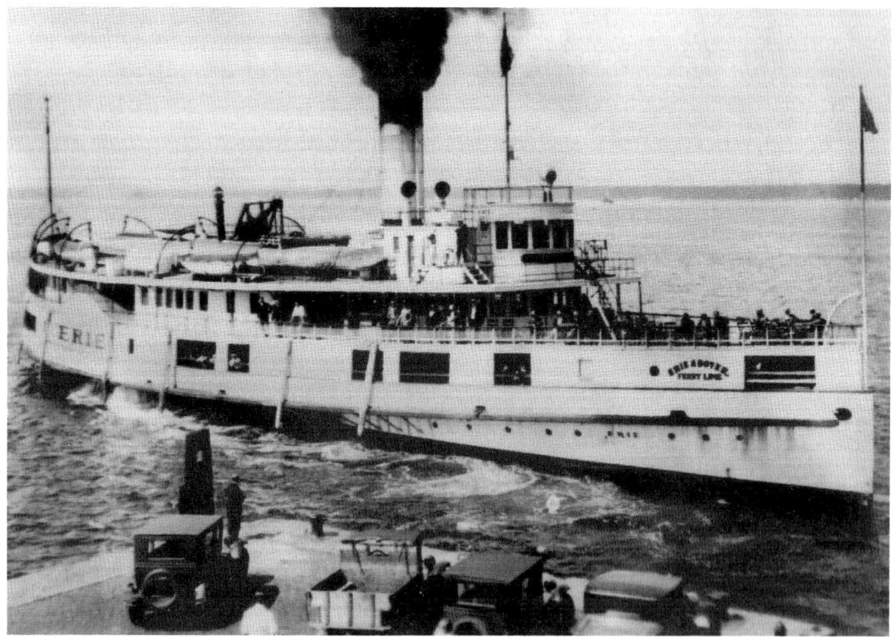

The *Erie*, one of Nicholson's ferries, at Erie. *Courtesy of Jerry Skrypzak.*

All thirty crew members took to the water to avoid the scalding-hot steel hull and burning deck. Help came from shore when onlookers spotted the flames, but by the time rescue boats arrived, three of the crew had perished. The burning hull was towed to shore near Dunkirk, where the flames were extinguished the next morning.

Sensing an opening in the Erie market, Detroit businessman William Nicolson launched a specialty Erie–Port Dover ferry service the following year, which continued until the Depression in 1931. In addition to the ferry service, the Nicholson ships featured moonlight cruises. The Nicholson ferry service peaked in 1929, when there were two ships in continuous service. The Nicholson line used three ships during six years of service—*Erie*, *Dover* and *Keystone*—and featured automobile ferry service between the two ports for an additional fee. In August 1929, the *Keystone* came close to a disaster when its engines stopped working in high winds, and it almost went aground on the tip of Long Point. Fortunately, several fish tugs came to its assistance and towed it back to Port Dover.

Pterodactyl (1926): Yachts Can Be Shipwrecks Too

There have been few recorded open-water shipwrecks of pleasure yachts on Lake Erie. This is largely because yachtsmen rarely find themselves required to cross the open waters of the lake at dangerous times like commercial sailors and fishermen. Pleasure boaters usually avoid storms and often put their boats away before the fall storm season. It is also important to note that as the number of pleasure boats began its geometric increase during the twentieth century, technologies that were not available to early commercial ships became commonplace. A simple thing like a ship-to-shore radio serves as an interesting example—the long-missing car-ferry *Marquette & Bessemer No. 2* did not have such a simple device. Improvements in weather forecasting have also helped. These days, a quick check of any television or Internet weather resource can warn boaters days or weeks in advance of approaching low-pressure systems. It is difficult to imagine an era when weather warnings consisted of sets of flags flown at Coast Guard Stations in major ports signaling fair weather, high wind or impending gales.

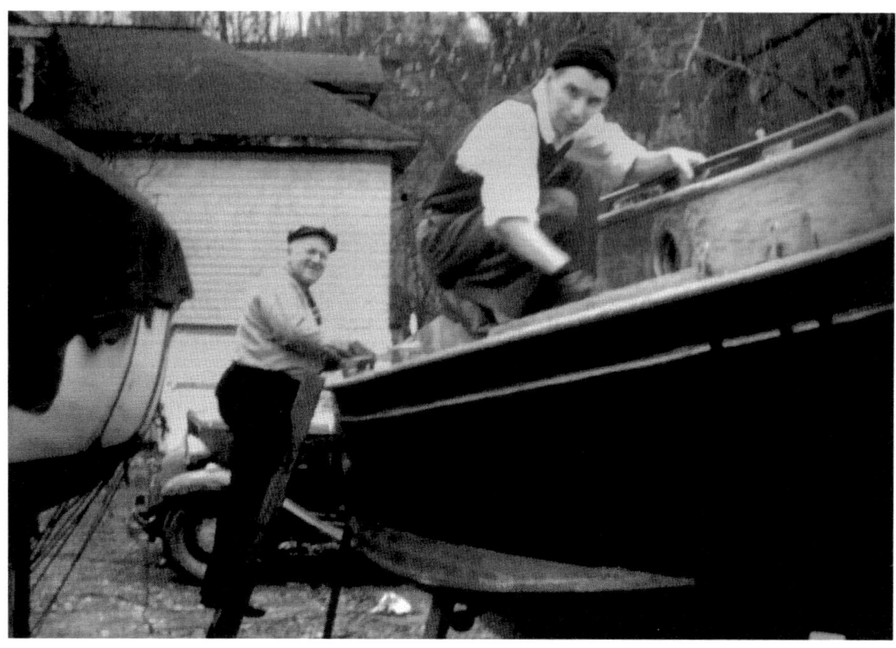

Byron Cooley (left), some years after his escape from near death, working on a boat at the Erie Yacht Club. *Courtesy of Erie Yacht Club.*

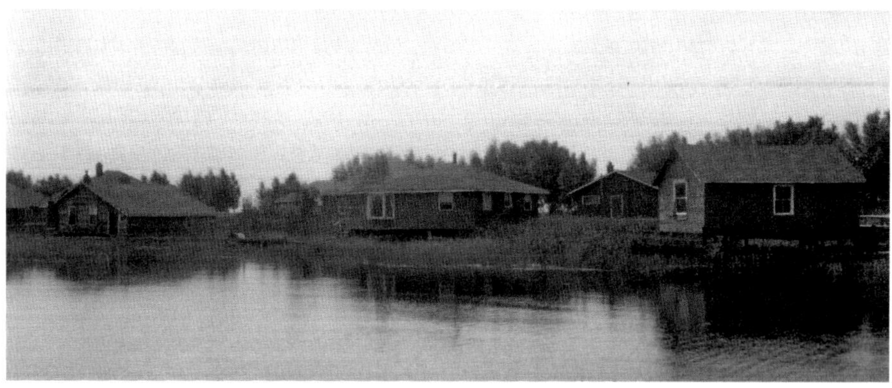

The cabins at Gravelly Bay. *Photograph by David Frew.*

Blame the industrial revolution. Shortened workweeks and regular hours allowed time for recreation, and boating exploded, often beginning with fishing. People were lured to the water in search of Lake Erie's abundant fish, an important source of protein for working-class families. But fishermen stayed relatively close to shore, and it was rare for a storm to result in a sinking or drowning. Offshore trips were most often attempted by sailors rather than power boaters, and the prime motivators were yacht clubs and their regattas. Lake Erie's yacht clubs began to appear in the late 1800s and were often connected as stopovers for long-distance major sailboat races, an activity that originated in New England. By 1900, there were Lake Erie yacht clubs in Buffalo, Erie, Cleveland, Detroit and Port Dover, and organized regattas connected them.

The Erie Yacht Club was established in 1895 as a sailing club. As membership grew, middle-class members began to launch and maintain sailboats of many sizes. One of the Erie Yacht Club's iconic characters was a man named Byron Cooley, who was not wealthy by any stretch of the imagination, but he was a great sailor who learned the ropes at the club by crewing on large yachts that competed in major regattas. Cooley eventually patched together his own yacht, a wooden twenty-four-footer called *Pterodactyl*. Those who recall Cooley's beloved yacht describe it as a hybrid created with leftover boat parts and jury-rigged equipment. It was largely held together by the varnish that Cooley lovingly applied to the brightwork each spring when he launched *Pterodactyl*.

For Erie sailors, Long Point, Ontario, just across the lake, represents an irresistible lure. The huge wilderness peninsula provides miles of secluded anchorages, and its north beaches are generally sheltered from Lake Erie's prevailing southwesterly winds. It is also an easy sail, lying at a broad reach from Erie's channel. For Ben Cooley there was an even more inviting reason to sail to Long Point: friends he had met while crewing on sailing regattas at Port Dover.

During the early history of Long Point, surveying errors resulted in a small area near the tip of the point and lighthouse compound that was not included in the 1867 purchase by the Long Point Company. Consequently, there were a few privately owned cabins on the east end of the peninsula near an inlet called Gravelly Bay, an anchorage used by boats seeking shelter from the open lake. On the weekend of August 20, 1926, Byron Cooley and his friend George Stickle departed for the cabins at Gravelly Bay. Taking a Friday off work, they enjoyed a blustery summer sail, arriving at Gravelly Bay to enjoy a weekend with friends.

On Sunday, when Cooley and Stickle had hoped to return to Erie, they awoke to the thrashing of high winds through cottonwood trees behind the cottages. After breakfast, they hiked east to the tip of the point to observe conditions on the lake, and what they saw was disturbing. Hoping for blue skies between Long Point and Erie, they were disappointed to see high waves, nasty white caps and threatening gray clouds. That was when Byron Cooley made the classic error that has created danger for more than a few sailors. Anxious to return to Erie and their jobs, especially after taking Friday off, Cooley and Stickle decided to try the return trip. Impatience versus prudence: a dilemma that has often been solved incorrectly. Their Long Point friends urged them to stay, but they departed, rounding the tip of Long Point and crashing into ten-foot waves on the return trip to Erie.

The geography of Lake Erie makes a return trip from Long Point to Erie much more difficult that the sail from Erie. The tack back is a close reach, during which sails are hardened and the prevailing current and waves are met head on—a "beat," as sailors refer to it. And the smaller and more fragile the sailing ship, the more difficult and dangerous such a beat becomes, as Cooley and Stickle were about to learn.

The twenty-five-mile open-lake crossing from Long Point to Erie in a boat the size of *Pterodactyl* should ordinarily take six or seven hours, but on that fated Sunday, twelve hours of frustrating tacking found the twosome well east of Long Point, less than halfway across the lake and suffering from significant leeway. Their tiny boat was being swept north and east by the current and waves at a more rapid rate than it was making headway toward Erie. Cooley and Stickle were tacking back and forth in mid-lake in huge breaking waves, and as they did, *Pterodactyl*'s seams were opening, and the tiny ship was taking on water.

Finally, after fifteen frustrating hours of tacking through enormous waves and making little headway, they decided to return to Long Point and seek shelter. Unfortunately, on their last easterly tack, while sailing parallel to the south beaches and a few miles west of the tip of the point, *Pterodactyl* took a large breaking wave across its cockpit and slipped below the water.

One minute Cooley and Stickle were steering *Pterodactyl* along the beaches of Long Point a mile offshore and the next they were swimming for their lives. Both men quickly realized that their only chance for survival was to swim to the beach at Long Point, but the current and waves were sweeping them rapidly to the east. If they failed to make it to the beaches before they were swept past the tip of the point, they would almost certainly die. Fortunately, they were both excellent swimmers, and they immediately set about the task of swimming as fast as they could, aiming northwest as they were being swept to the east.

It was a race against time, and for a while, it seemed that they would not make it. Cooley and Stickle swam as hard as they could, but the current was relentlessly moving them along the beaches to the east; it was beginning to seem like they would be driven past the tip of the point. Long Point is known for its monstrous waves, extreme currents and riptides. Then, at the last moment, a rogue current swept them north, where they were able to stand up on a sand bar that extended almost half a mile beyond the tip of Long Point. In a bit of irony, the swimmers were saved by the same sandbars that had claimed so many ships over the years. Cooley and Stickle waded to shore, walked back to the cabin where their Ontario friends were still playing cards and received dry clothing and food. A few days later, an American sailboat that had waited behind Long Point for the storm to end took them back to Erie.

Pterodactyl remains at the bottom of Lake Erie near Long Point.

HOWARD S GERKIN (1926): DANGERS OF DREDGING

The summer storm that claimed *Pterodactyl* proved fatal for an Erie workboat, a sand dredge named *Howard S Gerkin*. Sand and other dredged aggregates were big business on the Great Lakes. Construction, concrete and factory (tool-making) businesses required raw aggregate, and companies like Gerkin Sand & Gravel regularly sent dredges into Lake Erie's shallows to vacuum (dredge) materials. The aggregate materials were unloaded on shore and sold from the downtown docks—hence the typical piles of sand and gravel on Great Lakes waterfronts. Having a long, cumbersome suction tube with hoses connected to the lake bottom could place a ship—especially one that was less than seaworthy, as many of the old-time dredging ships were—at considerable risk.

The *Howard S Gerkin* was a 241-foot, 1,320-ton steel steamship that had been repurposed for dredging by the Gerkin Sand & Gravel Company of Buffalo. It was launched as the *Rosamund Billette* in 1910 as a bulk transport ship in the Red River and later moved to the Great Lakes. Its 41-foot beam was ideal for dredging since it provided a large carrying capacity, but it also put it at risk in high seas. It was designed for rivers, where the excessive

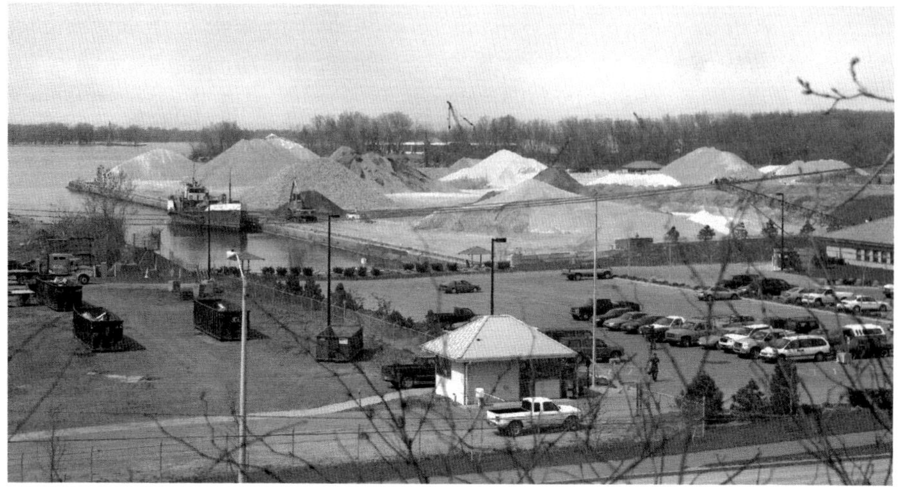

Erie's sand and gravel docks were serviced by sand dredges like the *Howard S Gerkin*. The dredge shown here is the *St. John*. *Photograph by Jerry Skrypzak.*

beam was not a liability. A deck-mounted steam shovel further decreased its seaworthiness, but the Gerkin Company was cautious, taking it out only in moderate weather and carefully metering runs into the open lake.

On August 21, 1926, the *Gerkin* and its crew of twenty were caught in the sudden and violent storm that took *Pterodactyl* to the bottom near Long Point. Dredging nine miles north of Erie on a direct course between Erie's Channel and the tip of Long Point, the ship was suddenly overpowered by a series of rogue waves that flooded the deck and swamped the massive open hold. The impact of the waves was exacerbated by the fact that the ship was anchored to the bottom by its dredging apparatus.

As the *Gerkin* was wallowing and about to sink, sixteen men took to two standard lifeboats, while four others launched a fourteen-foot rowing dingy. Before abandoning ship, the crew ignited a signal fire on the deck, piling almost everything that was combustible into a huge stack. Then they waited, hoping that someone would come to their rescue.

The crew members in the lifeboats were rescued by the car-ferry *Maitland*, but the four men in the captain's rowing dory had drifted so far from the site of the sinking that the rescuers could not locate them. A massive search was launched the next morning, and miraculously, Herman Wagerman was spotted swimming on a wave top by the crew of an Erie Coast Guard cutter. The other three men from the fourteen-foot boat perished. Wagerman was returned to the Erie Coast Guard station in hypothermic condition. He later said that the small rowing dory overturned in the huge waves and that only he and Bill Logan came to the surface. Logan and Wageman swam for hours as they were carried offshore by southerly winds. Eventually, Logan slipped beneath the surface and disappeared. The overturned dory was recovered in eastern Lake Erie a few days later.

Confusion over the precise location of the sinking kept divers from finding the *Howard S Gerkin*. Some of the confusion was caused by Mr. Gerkin himself, who was aboard the sandsucker on the evening of the tragedy. Gerkin unsuccessfully tried to sue the Erie Coast Guard for not coming to the aid of his ship after the crew had launched flares. In making his case, he claimed that he was well west of the site where the wreck actually took place and within clear sight of Erie's Coast Guard station. Given the actual wreck site, which was located by Mary Howard in 1996, there was no way that the Erie Coast Guard could have seen the *Gerkin* or its signals.

PART VI
MODERN FISHING DISASTERS

The Explosion of the *Mary Lou* (1952): They Should Have Switched to Diesel

Commercial fishing is dangerous. There have always been frightening stories of stoic fishermen setting off at 4:00 a.m. to risk life and limb for whitefish, perch or pickerel. But one of Lake Erie's most tragic losses did not involve heavy seas, icy squalls or collisions at sea. It was a freak accident at the Erie dock in 1952. By the 1950s, there was a wholesale transition from gasoline engines to diesel.

Gasoline leaks had caused dozens of explosions and fires, and diesel engines essentially eliminated those dangers. The problem with diesels, however, was that they were expensive. Aboard the *Mary Lou*, a fifty-two-foot gill netter in Erie, Captain Jim Peterson was tempted, but instead of installing a new diesel, he purchased a second gasoline engine identical to the one already in his tug. Gasoline engines were relatively inexpensive, and Peterson reasoned that he could have the second engine rebuilt and serviced during off seasons and begin each year with a refurbished and reliable engine. He knew that his solution was not as good as a new diesel, but fishing was beginning to slow, and he reasoned that a rebuilt engine each year would eliminate most of the dangers associated with gasoline.

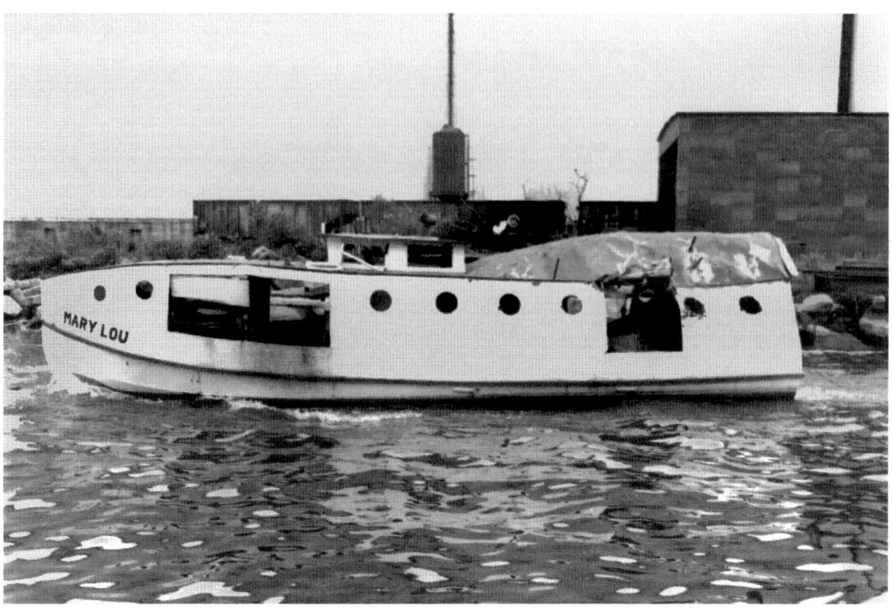

Mary Lou after the explosion. *Photograph by Al Taylor.*

At 5:00 a.m. on August 13, Peterson was in the wheelhouse trying to start his engine, while the crew prepared *Mary Lou* for the day's run. Peterson nudged the main switch into the *on* position, hit the ignition and heard a disappointing *click*. It was then that he remembered a pesky loose cable on the main engine battery under the covered engine compartment inside the aft cabin. Peterson opened the wheelhouse door and yelled for a crew member to get a wrench and tighten the battery connections. It was not the first time loose battery cables had frustrated the crew that year. Peterson had purchased new cable ends, but he had not had time to install them. Not a big problem for the crew, however, since a quick twist of a crescent wrench was all that was needed to make contact.

"Ready, Cap?" a crew member yelled while leaning into the below-deck engine compartment. Thumbing the wrench down after he had positioned it on the positive battery terminal, however, the crew member lost his grip on the engine companionway where he was balancing himself. When he instinctively used his free hand to stabilize himself, the wrench dropped across the battery, where it contacted the negative battery terminal. A sharp *crack* reverberated as the wrench shorted the battery. It was a sound that had been heard countless times as careless mechanics worked with metal tools around battery banks. But somehow, this time was different. This crack was louder, more ominous, and was followed by a deep, resonant echo. It was also the first time that such a careless event had taken place after thousands of square feet of oil-soaked gill nets had spent an evening closed inside the aft compartment of a fish tug.

The noise and accompanying spark paused for a moment and then moved upward in slow motion. Instead of dissipating after a millisecond, it grew into an explosive flash that pulsated as it rose toward the metal cabin interior. Mesmerized by the light show emanating from the bank of batteries, the wrench-juggling crew member lost his balance and fell headfirst into the engine compartment. And just as he did, the slow-motion pyrotechnic display in the center of the boat picked up speed and transformed itself into a brilliant flash of yellow light that took on the intensity of a bolt of lightning during an August storm.

Dockside observers reported seeing a plume of fire rocketing from amidships. The original burst of blinding light was followed by an intense explosion that threw a crew member who had been preparing net boxes into the air and smashed his body like a hapless rag doll against the stern rail, killing him instantly. Captain Peterson was lifted from his wheelhouse seat and thrown through the windshield onto the bow of the tug. Fortunately, the crewman who had slipped headfirst into the engine room was saved from the force of the explosion.

The force of the blast threw sleeping firemen from their beds at the stationhouse a mile away. When the stunned firemen rushed to the docks a short time later, Captain Peterson was unconscious and bleeding profusely on the bow of *Mary Lou*, the crew member who had been impaled on *Mary Lou*'s stern was dead and the man who had fallen into the engine compartment was wandering the dock in a state of shock. Peterson was taken to Hamot Hospital, where he was treated for burns and a concussion. He remained in critical condition for several days, and it was weeks before he regained his hearing. Peterson was eventually released and recovered, but the explosion made him reconsider his life as a fisherman. Times had become difficult for fishermen, and worst of all, Captain Peterson's son, John, who had earned a finance degree at the University of Pittsburgh, had returned to Erie to take a job with Erie Insurance so that he would be close to his family and able help out on the tugs. What if he had been aboard that morning? John Peterson had grown up working in the fishing business and earned his way through school by helping on his father's fish tug.

Peterson sent his wounded tug to Erie's Paasch Boat Yard, which made it seaworthy. When Paasch was finished, *Mary Lou* was towed to Port Dover's

Gamble Shipyard, where it was rebuilt and sold. Peterson retired from fishing and encouraged his son to concentrate on his career in the insurance business. When Captain Peterson's son retired in 1990, he left an "unusual legacy," considering that it was made possible by the son of a commercial fisherman. He donated $7 million to his undergraduate alma mater, the University of Pittsburgh, for the John and Gertrude Peterson Athletic Center, where generations of Pitt Panther fans will continue to watch basketball and other indoor events thanks to Lake Erie and commercial fishing.

Richard R (1954): Extending the Season

The 1950s were troubling times for commercial fishermen. Blue pike were literally disappearing; herring were becoming rare; and the perch, yellow pike and whitefish catches were in decline. Commercial fishermen were desperate to increase their catch totals, and two traditional tricks that had been used to increase revenue were (1) to continue fishing into the winter (December and January) months and (2) to move their fish tugs west in an effort to get an early spring start the following season. Since the prevailing current and wind on Lake Erie move from southwest to northeast, pushing the winter ice, having a tug in an Ohio port would allow a fisherman to get an early start on the next fishing season when the fish were running.

In December 1954, the Rogalas of Erie moved their fish tug, the *Richard R*, west in preparation for the 1955 season. It was near the end of the blue pike era, and Captain Frank Rogala; his brother, Richard; and crew member Russell Smith were planning to winter the *Richard R* west of Erie in Conneaut or Ashtabula. En route, they had found a productive trap netting spot just a few miles offshore between the two Ohio ports and decided to do some late-season fishing. With the tug berthed in Conneaut, Ohio, they had been commuting to tend their nets every other day and bringing the fish back to Erie.

On December 21, the three men left Erie at 5:00 a.m. and drove to Conneaut. By 6:00 a.m., they were clearing Conneaut Harbor in their diesel-powered, forty-five-foot, welded-steel fish tug. The *Richard R* was built in Erie by the Barcelona Fish Company in 1939 and was known as a reliable and powerful tug. The tug's reputation, combined with the fact that people in Conneaut knew that the Rogalas were not planning to continue as

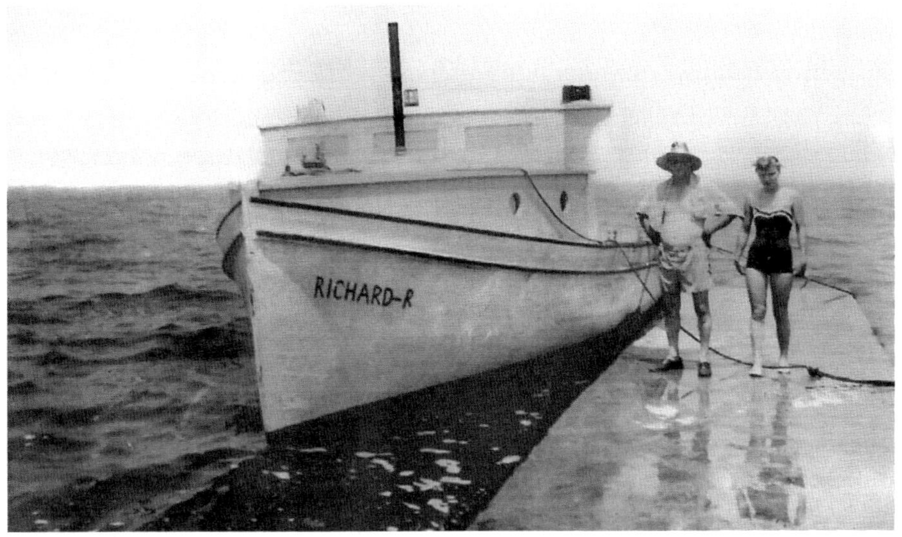

The *Richard R* after it was recovered. *Courtesy of the Rogala family.*

permanent residents, dissuaded their dock neighbors from being concerned when the weather turned ugly that morning after the tug had departed. By noon, the northwesterly wind had risen from five to more than thirty miles per hour. When the *Richard R* failed to return, dockside observers assumed that it had either returned to Erie or moved west to Ashtabula. But when no one retrieved the Rogalas' truck for two days, concern grew.

In Erie, Frank Rogala's father, Dan, was worried. His sons would not have disappeared for two days without a phone call. On December 24, Dan Rogala led a search party onto the lake. Using a Conneaut salvage tug, he went to the spot where his sons had reported that their nets were set and found the *Richard R*'s net markers. The pattern of the floating markers seemed disturbed, and Dan Rogala began to suspect that the *Richard R* might have sunk during the storm while the nets were being tended. Mr. Rogala returned to Conneaut to hire divers and search for the tug, but the holiday season and a week of poor weather prevented divers from entering the water.

On January 5, 1955, Dan Rogala was finally able to return to the site of the nets with salvage tugs. Using steel cables and grappling hooks, he and the salvers worked a pattern around and through the nets until one of the hooks contacted a large, heavy object. After attaching additional lines, the salvagers began lifting the target to the surface. An hour of winching and adjusting angles of the lines brought the gunnels of the *Richard R* to the surface. Mystery solved. Salvers marked the *Richard R* and tried to straighten it so that they could pump it out and bring it back to Conneaut, but the weather worsened, and the submerged tug slipped back under the water. The salvers were able to see, however, that the *Richard R* had a partially spooled net on its retrieval winch, suggesting that the crew was in the midst of retrieving nets when a wave breached the aft section and the tug sank in a following sea. Convinced that the crew might either be on the *Richard R* or tangled in the maze of netting, Dan Rogala left the nets in place and returned to Erie for divers. On January 15, divers found the body of Captain Frank Rogala tangled in a net. The other two crew members were never recovered.

Aletha B (1974) and *Stanley Clipper* (1984): Troubles with Trawling

Lake Erie's rainbow smelt is not a native species. Smelt were introduced to Lake Michigan in 1912 to support sports angling and quickly spread to the other Great Lakes. By the 1950s, they had exploded in Lake Erie. Anglers were happily catching them by the thousands, but biologists were concerned with their uncontrolled expansion and were trying to determine the impact of the smelt on the troubled Lake Erie food chain. University studies revealed that the carnivorous little fish, which had probably destroyed the blue pike, was devastating newly hatched perch and walleye and devouring the lower end of the food chain. Doomsday scenarios began to describe a lake essentially devoid of any other species.

The international Lake Erie Committee initiated a test program designed to simultaneously control smelt and provide a source of income for commercial fishermen. As a part of the control initiative, the Ontario Ministry of Natural Resources (OMNR) began a trawling program in 1952 designed to catch enough smelt to keep the population in check. Offering grant money to fishermen who would purchase special smelt licenses, the OMNR hired shrimp fishermen from Biloxi, Mississippi, to teach Ontario fishermen to rig their fish tugs and drag (trawl) for smelt.

Trawling involves pulling a huge net through schools of smelt until the trailing end is filled and then lifting the catch into the tug with winches and an A-Frame. Like other commercially harvested species in Ontario,

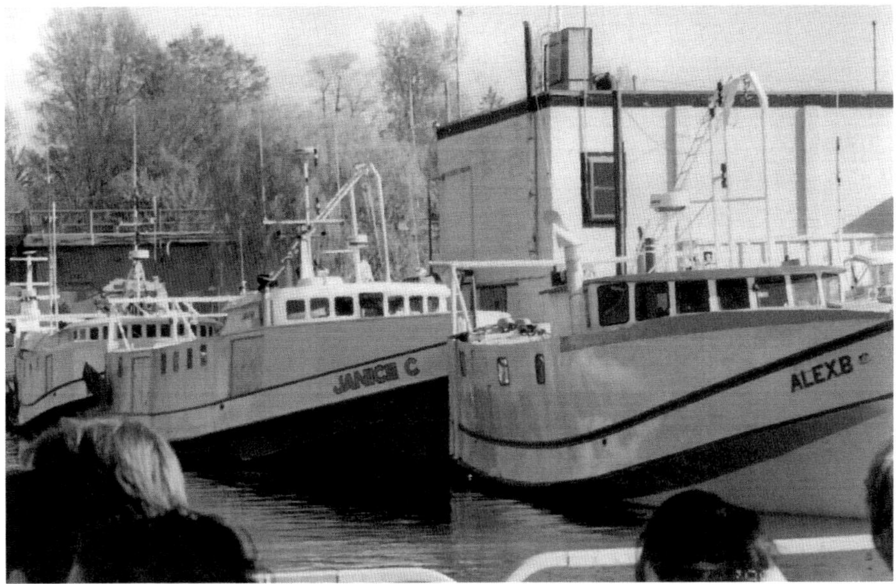

Port Dover fish tugs rigged with A-Frames and metal doors for trawling. *Photograph by David Frew.*

an annual smelt quota is set (in quarterly increments) and adjusted each year as biologists make statistical observations of the Lake Erie population. Commercial fishermen in Ontario, who had been experiencing reduced catches of perch, yellow pickerel (walleye) and whitefish, relished the opportunity to make additional use of their tugs and equipment. Most continued to purchase gill netting licenses and added trawling as a secondary venture. Clever marketing found lucrative niches for processed smelt, the most interesting of which was as a sushi product exported to Japan. There was an unsuccessful attempt to begin trawling in Erie, but bottom conditions were unsuitable.

The technical requirements of trawling are tricky. Two large sliding doors are deployed in smooth areas of lake bottom. If the nets are tangled on irregularities, they can be ripped or lost on bottom structures. These "hook-ups" are the bane of trawlers. A second problem is the accidental capture of other species. The only species trawlers are allowed to catch are smelt or incidental "rough" fish. Since Ontario's commercial fishermen are inspected each time they return to port, "high value fish," including perch, walleye or whitefish, have to be pre-prepared and handed over to the OMNR if they are netted. In practical terms, a retrieved trawl net that contains an appreciable number of perch, whitefish or walleye represents a significant problem. The fish can't be returned to the water since a sudden net pull to the surface from depths of one hundred feet bursts their swim bladders.

The new smelt catch proved highly profitable. In just the second year of trawling, Ontario fishermen harvested more than 1 million pounds. While Ontario's fishing community did not particularly like the new product, people resigned themselves to the fact that their work was controlling a nuisance fish that had been threatening desirable species. They also enjoyed the extra profits that were earned by adding trawling to their gill netting licenses, and by the mid-1980s, smelt trawling had become a Port Dover way of life.

Between 1970 and 1980, Lake Erie catch data began to reverse itself. The total catch, which had been falling, suddenly increased, but during the same period, the total catch value fell. The cause of this apparent contradiction was a new catch category called "rendering." Fishermen had become aware of the opportunity to sell unregulated junk fish to processors for use as ground fish meal, oils and other agricultural products. Demand for fish meal was increasing because of catfish farmers in the American South who didn't care what kind of fish went into the production of the feed that they were using. The opportunity to harvest fish for rendered products provided a new source of revenue for Ontario's trawlers. Before or after completing their quotas, fishermen could extend their seasons by trawling for junk fish. Why not add new ways to deploy underutilized investment capital?

While the trawling business has added to the Canadian commercial fishing industry, it has also proved dangerous. Dragging heavy trawls through the water places fish tugs at risk, and the dangers of early and late-season fishing are increased. On Sunday, March 24, 1974, the new owners of Port Dover's *Aletha B* decided to go trawling for mooneyes, an unregulated rough fish. Alan and Wayne Perry were relatively inexperienced, having grown up on a farm just north of Port Dover, but the spring smelt quota was not due to go into effect until April 1, and there were bills to be paid. Given their farm-bred work ethic, the Perrys were pacing the docks, anxious to start fishing, and they had heard that mooneyes were running along the north beaches of Long Point. Thinking that they could use some practice in advance of the April smelt run, the Perrys followed Captain Terry Hagen's *Trimac* out into Long Point Bay. With just two aboard, they were shorthanded, but they were not sure how much their junk fish catch would bring, and they were trying to save money.

Schooling mooneyes are easy to spot. They swim near the surface, breaking the water in visible patterns, and within an hour, *Trimac*'s crew had located them. The mooneyes were heading from the colder waters of the open lake into the relative warmth of Long Point Bay. The Perrys quickly lowered their trawl net and began moving parallel with *Trimac*. Terry Hagen and his first mate, Jim Lindsay, had been generous mentors to the Perrys, helping the converted farm boys with everything from equipment to navigation and tug maintenance. When *Aletha B* followed *Trimac* out into Long Point Bay, Captain Hagen was on the radio offering continuous support. At 3:00 p.m., the wind picked up dramatically, and Terry Hagen called to see how *Aletha B* was doing. Alan Perry responded that they were catching huge loads with each run. A few minutes later, however, Hagen received a distress call from Alan, who said that they were in trouble. Hagen lifted his net and headed for the last place where he had seen the *Aletha B*, and thirty minutes later, he spotted it floating upside down. A few hours later, a Canadian Coast Guard cutter arrived at the site of the stricken *Aletha B*, which Hagen had marked with a buoy before it sunk. The cutter called for a helicopter, and a systematic search was conducted for the Perrys, with no success.

Aletha B was salvaged from 90 feet of water several days later, returned to Port Dover, rebuilt and returned to fish for the 1975 season. A Coast Guard investigation concluded that *Aletha B*, which had a shallow draft of only 3.3 feet, was overloaded and unstable in the growing waves. *Triamac*, by contrast, was 58 feet long with a draft of 4.5 feet. In a stunning coincidence, almost two years later, another set of brothers recovered the bodies of the Perrys while fishing from two different tugs. Chuck Scott found Dale Perry from the *Dover Rose* while trawling in June 1976, and one month later, his brother, Vinny, found the body of Wayne Perry while fishing from the *M&K*.

On April 30, 1984, the sixty-foot *Stanley Clipper* left Port Dover at 5:00 a.m. in the company of another fish tug, the *Ciscoette*, and headed for the tip of Long Point. Both the *Stanley Clipper* and *Ciscoette* were mid-1930s welded-steel tugs. *Ciscoette*—which was ten feet longer, two tons heavier and carried an additional foot of draft—had been built by the Gamble Yard in Port Dover. Both tugs were working for Misner Fisheries Limited.

Smelt had been running on the south side of Long Point, and Captain James Saunders and his crew of John Mummery and Daryl Clement settled in for the long ride to the end of the point. By 7:30 a.m., both tugs were around the point with their nets down. Fishing was good, and by 11:00 a.m., Captain Saunders had radioed the *Ciscoette* to say that since the wind was beginning to increase and they had nearly filled their totes with smelt, they were heading back. Within half an hour, *Ciscoette* raised its last net and was following *Stanley Clipper* home.

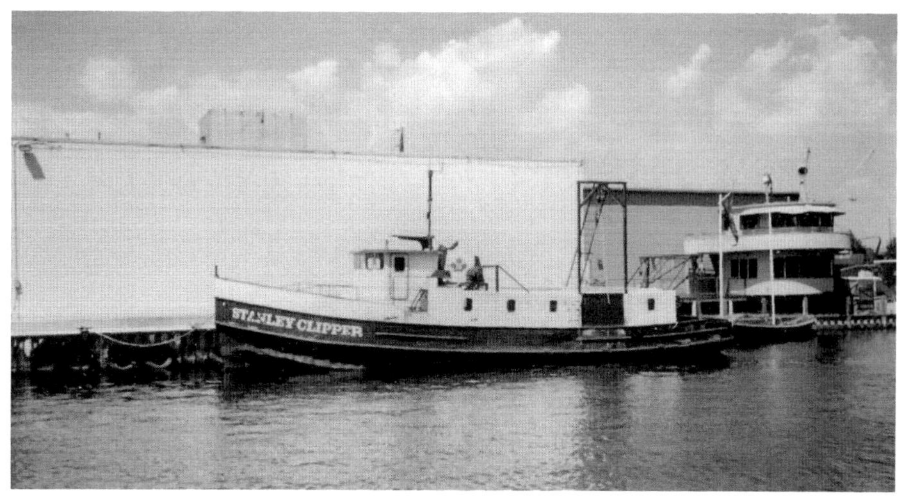

Stanley Clipper at the Port Dover docks after it was recovered. *Photograph by David Frew.*

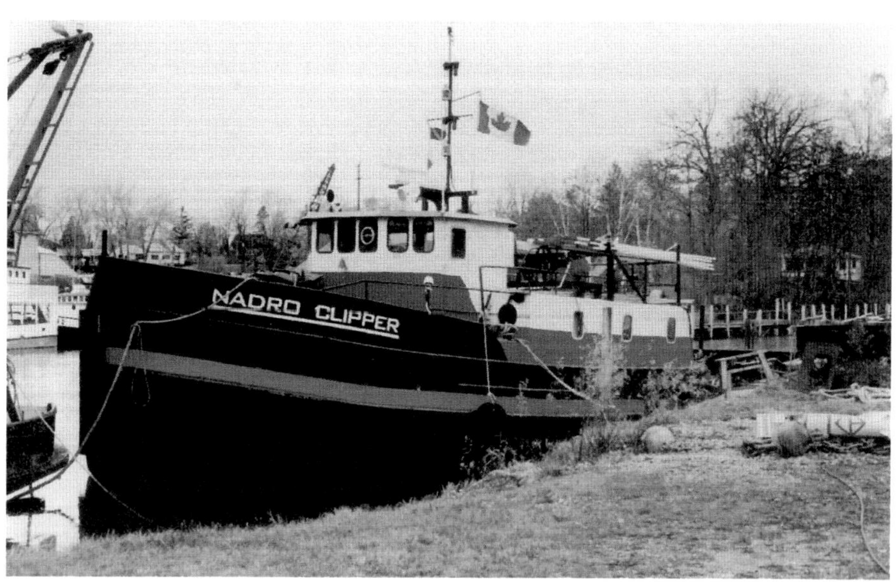

The *Nadro Clipper*. *Courtesy of Bill Nadrofsky, Nadro Marine, Port Dover.*

By the time the tugs had rounded Long Point and begun the fifteen-mile trek across Long Point Bay to Port Dover, however, the wind had reached forty knots, and the waves were building. At 1:00 p.m., instruments aboard *Ciscoette* were reading wind gusts of seventy knots, and the radar screen showed the *Stanley Clipper* tacking off to the west to dampen the impact of the growing waves. *Ciscoette* was only two miles behind the *Stanley Clipper*, but its crew could not see the other tug in the blinding spray and rain. By 1:30 p.m., fifteen-foot waves had prompted the *Ciscoette* to follow the *Stanley Clipper*'s lead and begin tacking back and forth across the waves. At 2:00 p.m., in the midst of a tacking maneuver during which *Ciscoette* was shifting from a western heading to the east, a twenty-five-foot wave struck the tug head, shattering the wheelhouse windows and ripping the radar antenna off the roof.

At 2:15 p.m., the grim silence aboard *Ciscoette* was interrupted by a Mayday call from the *Stanley Clipper*. *Ciscoette* immediately tacked west to try to render aid, but with near-zero visibility and no radar, the men aboard were just guessing as they pounded through heavy seas toward the position where they had last seen their friends on the radar screen. *Ciscoette* searched until dark, struggling in huge waves. They were eventually joined by a Canadian Coast Guard rescue ship and three other Port Dover fish tugs, but all they found was debris from the sinking.

Three days later, the sunken fish tug was located by salvage tugs in thirty-eight feet of water near the north beaches of Long Point. The *Stanley Clipper* was raised and returned to Port Dover, where it languished at the docks for years, serving to memorialize the dangers of commercial fishing. The bodies of all three crew members eventually floated to the surface and were recovered in June and August of that year.

Port Dover's Nadro Marine Services ignored a timeless maritime tradition that would have suggested that a sunken vessel would be doomed to bad fortune and purchased the old fish tug, converting it to a work tug. The company renamed it *Nadro Clipper*.

PART VII
IS LAKE ERIE'S SHIPWRECK ERA OVER?

THE WHALEBACK *JAMES B COLGATE* (1916): HURRICANE SEASONS PAST

Several historic storms contend for the title of Lake Erie's all-time worst, but from a historic perspective, the 1916 Black Friday Storm seems to be the winner. The 1913 White Hurricane may have been the greatest storm in the history of the Great Lakes, but its fury was focused on Lake Huron, where it took ten ships to the bottom and drove another twenty-three onshore. By the time the White Hurricane had passed east, however, it dealt only a glancing blow to Lake Erie. The most famous Lake Erie wreck spawned by the 1913 storm was the *Elpheke*, which took refuge behind Long Point. With his ship leaking badly on the night of the White Hurricane, *Elphike*'s captain drove his steamship aground west of the Long Point Lighthouse so that he and his crew could wade to the safety of the shore.

The Friday the thirteenth Black Friday Storm in 1916, arriving three years after the sinking of *Elpheke*, was a focused Lake Erie disturbance. It was also a surprise to most of the ships caught in it since, unlike the 1913 White Hurricane, there were few warnings. While Coast Guard stations from Duluth to Detroit had been flying storm warning flags before the 1913 eruption, the Friday the thirteenth disturbance in 1916 seemed to pop up at the last

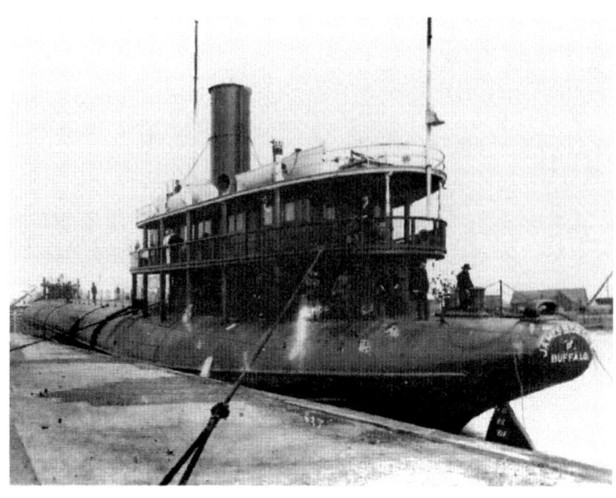

The whaleback steamship *James B Colgate*. *Courtesy of Jerry Skrypzak.*

minute, taking many by complete surprise. A low-pressure system was stalled over Lake Erie, with its barometric center located north of Cleveland. But that low pressure, by itself, was not significant. Remembering the relatively recent events of 1913, however, several ships waited on Thursday, October 12, 1916, and watched the barometer sink to a record low.

Unbeknownst to them, Lake Erie's rogue low-pressure cell was about to be joined by two new storms. A Gulf of Mexico hurricane that had terrorized people in Louisiana, Mississippi and Texas re-formed and moved north through the Ohio Valley. The eye of that storm reorganized over Cincinnati, and with its power reenergized, the October 1916 Hurricane picked up speed and rushed north, reaching western Lake Erie on Thursday. Attracted like a magnet to the low-pressure cell that had stalled over the lake, the new arrival formed a double-eye that began to inch its way east. The double storm was forced to make a hard right turn when it banged into a third disturbance, an Alberta clipper that was racing south. When the three storms met over Lake Erie and joined atmospheric forces, they began to move slowly east—ever so slowly. Lake Erie's destiny was about to be defined by one of weather history's first "perfect storms."

On the west end of the lake, the 380-foot steamship *Merida* left the Detroit River for Buffalo. Observers said that *Merida*'s captain seemed to have second thoughts when he entered the open waters and that he tried to come about and return to the river, but his stern was lifted by a wave and the ship almost rolled. When last seen, *Merida* was steaming east and out of control in massive following seas, with waves that had risen to more than twenty-five feet. Two more ships were lost on the western end of the lake that day. The first was a schooner barge that was being towed by the Erie steam barge

Tempest. The *Tempest* had made the trip to the west end of the lake early Thursday towing the *D.L. Filer*, a 161-foot schooner barge. *Tempest*'s captain anchored his consort, the *D.L. Filer*, just west of the Detroit River and left to fetch a second barge from Toledo. Unfortunately for the *D.L. Filer* and its crew of seven, when the storm erupted on Thursday, the *Tempest* remained in Toledo, leaving the anchored consort to fend for itself. Meanwhile, the *Marshall Butters*, a 164-foot lumber hooker, also left the Detroit River on Thursday. As soon as the captain realized the size of the waves, he tried to come about, but a wave lifted the stern and rolled the *Butters* more than ninety degrees; the ship foundered.

On the east end of Lake Erie, the *James B Colgate*, a 308-foot "unsinkable whaleback," left Buffalo with a load of coal bound for the Detroit River and Thunder Bay shortly after midnight on the unlucky departure date, Friday the thirteenth. Like *Merida*, which was heading east, the westbound *Colgate* was never seen again. By Saturday, newspapers from Detroit to Buffalo were proclaiming the loss of four ships on Lake Erie. The *Butters* and *Filer* went down close enough to the Detroit River that witnesses saw what happened and went to the aid of their crews. All but one of the crew members aboard the *Butters* was lost as the schooner barge dragged its anchor all day Friday and finally sank in the shallows east of the river entrance. The crew climbed the two masts, but the foremast snapped, taking five men with it into the cold October water. By a miracle, the frozen captain was plucked, barely alive, from the mizzenmast by the passenger ship *Western States*. Thirteen crew members from the *Butters* were rescued by the steamship *Frank Billings.*

The *Merida* and *Colgate* simply disappeared. Two ships traveling in opposite directions along Lake Erie's busiest trade route just dropped out of sight. While the locations of the two steamships were shrouded in mystery until 1975 and 1993, respectively, when the wrecks of the *Merida* and then the *Colgate* were located, there was one survivor. Walter Grashaw, captain of the *Colgate*, was rescued after thirty-six hours hanging on to a tiny raft. Thanks to his testimony, we have a vivid account of the conditions on Lake Erie that night. Grashaw, who was picked up on Sunday morning by the railroad/car-ferry *Marquette & Bessemer No. 2 II* (a replacement ship for the lost *Marquette & Bessemer No. 2*), told reporters that the *Colgate* was immediately greeted by five-foot waves when it departed Buffalo. Since whalebacks were noted for their ability to run through heavy weather, however, Grashaw had no thoughts about turning back and continued toward Long Point, usually a seven-hour run. By 8:00 a.m., however, he was still not within sight of the Long Point Light, the wind was blowing

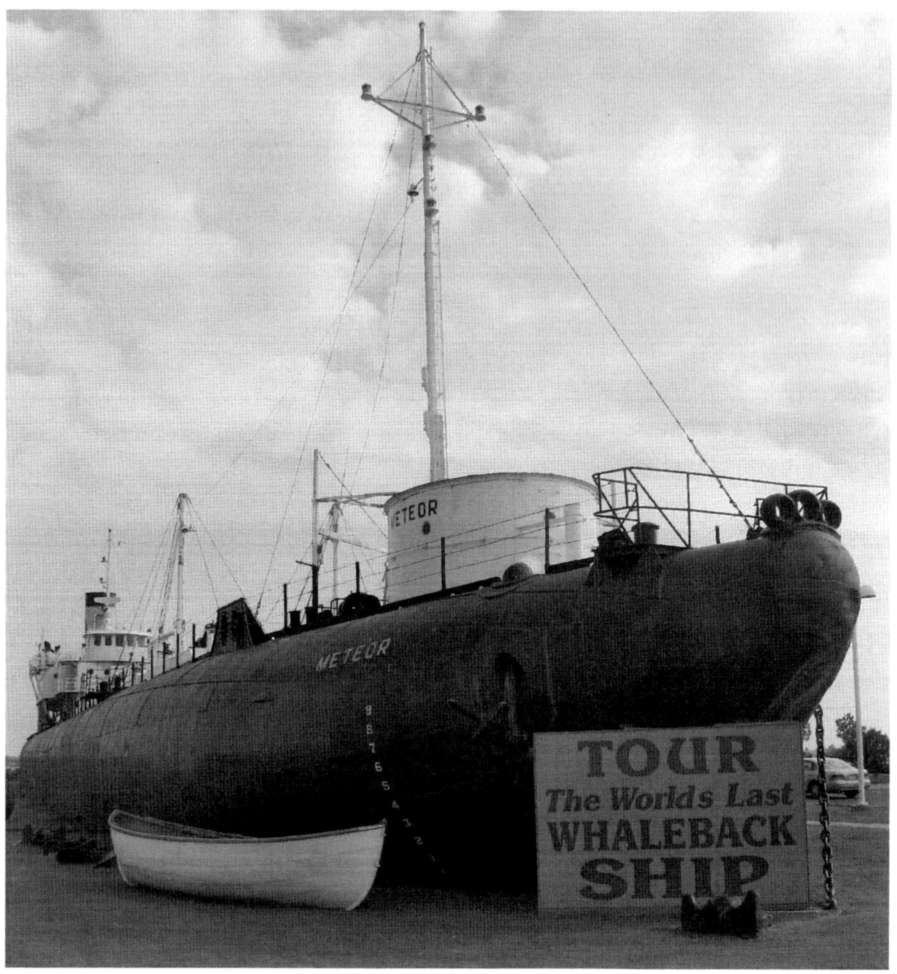

The *Meteor* (originally the *Rockefeller*) in Superior, Wisconsin. *Photograph by Jerry Skrypzak.*

fifty miles per hour and the ship was barely making headway against monstrous opposing waves. Twelve hours later, by Grashaw's estimate, winds had reached ninety miles per hour, with gusts going to one hundred. The *Colgate* was experiencing the full fury of the three-cell "perfect storm" that had exploded on Lake Erie, and it was just west of the base of Long Point, barely able to keep its bow to weather in forty- and fifty-foot waves running from the southwest.

The 1916 storm lingered for twenty hours on Lake Erie. Winds continuously blew from the southwest, and since wave heights are determined by wind velocity, fetch (linear distance across the surface of the water over which the wind is blowing) and the elapsed time that the wind blows, the 1916 waves had an opportunity to mature.

Captain Walter Grashaw, who spent thirty-six hours riding a tiny life raft through the 1916 Black Friday waves, reported crests as high as fifty feet, with breaking top water that sent his raft tumbling through several 360-degree rolls. He later said that if he had been in a traditional lifeboat instead of the ship's flat-bottomed maintenance raft, he would not have lasted an hour.

There is only one of the unique whaleback ships left, the *Meteor* (*Rockefeller*), which is preserved on dry land in Superior, Wisconsin, home of the inventor of the design, Robert McDougal.

Wreck Spotting on a Clear Day: What a Difference a Day Makes

During the years when I left academia to become executive director of Erie County Historical Society, we sponsored a fall lecture series entitled "Gales of November," which we held in our planetarium. The lectures were based on Quadrangle wrecks, and holding them under the stars, where we projected the evening skies at the time of the disasters, created excitement. One evening after I showed PowerPoint images illustrating the wreck of the steamer *Atlantic*, and as the crowd drifted away, one man remained to chat. After a brief introduction, he explained that he was an amateur pilot and reached into a folder for several photographs. There were pictures of his twenty-year-old airplane and a series of aerial photographs including Long Point, Presque Isle and the skyline of Erie.

"You will be interested in this," he said, pulling a final photograph from his folder. It seemed to be a picture of the surface of Lake Erie with a buoy in the center. "Know what that is?" he asked, pointing to a shadow that seemed attached to the marker buoy. I had no idea. "It's the steamer *Atlantic*," he proudly announced. "I have spotted it several times on clear days. And there are other visible wrecks, as well."

I stared at the shadow, mesmerized. I wanted to believe, but I was skeptical. Could the dark shadow in the photograph really be a shipwreck? Was it the *Atlantic*, more than 160 feet below the surface?

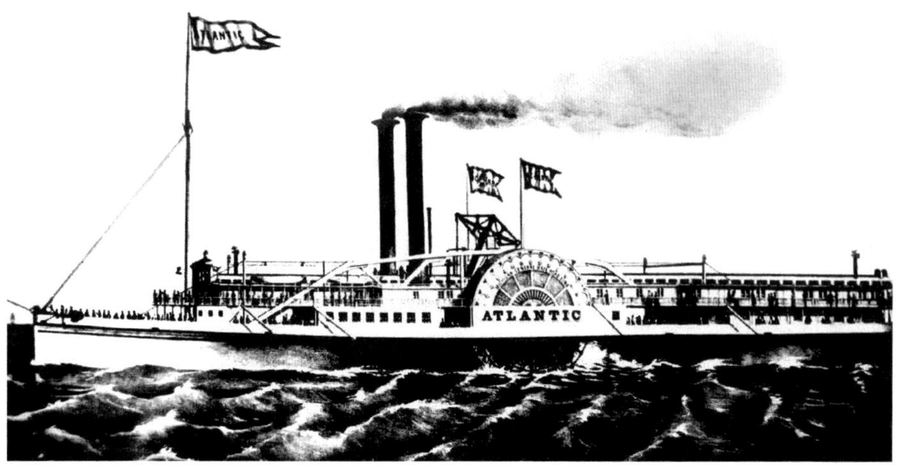

The height of the *Atlantic* off the bottom casts a large-enough shadow to be visible even though it is 165 feet below the surface. *Courtesy of Jerry Skrypzak.*

One of my former students, Kevin Karg, is a pilot who loves to fly over the lake. When I bumped into him a few weeks later, I broached the subject. I asked him if it seemed possible that deep-water wrecks could be so transparent. He nodded but admitted that he had never specifically gone on a wreck-hunting quest. Then he uttered the magic words: "Any time you want to go, just let me know."

On a crisp April day, following a week of light winds, we took off from the Erie Airport with binoculars, camera and the GPS coordinates for four shipwrecks: the *Rob Roy*, *Indiana* (Stone Wreck), *Atlantic* and *Dean Richmond*. It was a series of wreck locations that would lead us in a circle, beginning with a southwesterly trek along the lakeshore to the *Rob Roy*, west of the city. I had reasoned that if any of the shipwrecks would be visible from the air, it would be the *Rob Roy* since it was in relatively shallow water. From *Rob Roy*, we would fly northwest to the *Indiana* and then circle north toward Long Point and the *Atlantic*. Finally, we would make a long southerly loop toward the U.S. side of the lake and the *Dean Richmond*. Turning west from the site of the *Dean Richmond*, we would fly back along the lakeshore to the airport. It was quite a flight plan!

As a sailor used to six or seven knots of speed, I was psychologically prepared for a long ride. We were about to travel west of the city, across the lake in a gradual circle, east to the New York state line and return to Erie. Such a trip in a sailboat could take days. After the initial excitement of takeoff, we banked right and followed a course to the location of the *Rob Roy*, an old schooner barge that lies in less than thirty feet of water. I knew that the *Rob Roy* was there since I have visited the site and seen it myself. Faithfully following the course to the *Rob Roy*, we passed over the GPS location without seeing any indication of its remains. Disappointed, we circled for a second and then a third pass. No *Rob Roy*!

I was embarrassed for bringing my friend on what was beginning to seem like a wild goose chase, but he interrupted my apology by saying that he loved flying. Undaunted, we headed east for the *Indiana*, which lies in sixty feet of water. Again, there could be no doubt of its existence since it is Erie's most popular shipwreck dive site. Nearing the location, we spotted a white buoy that marked the location of the wreck, but again there was no visible sign from the air.

Disappointed again, we turned toward Long Point, a trip that takes four or five hours in a large sailboat. Moments later, we spotted Long Point's south beaches. Then we saw a marker buoy at the location of the wreck. We flew directly over the buoy, and there, like a magical apparition, we spotted it. The underwater shape of the steamer *Atlantic* appeared as vividly as if it had been lying in just a few feet of water. After the disappointment of not spotting the first wrecks, we were elated.

Two loops around the *Atlantic* and some pictures later, and we were off to our last shipwreck, the *Dean Richmond*, which lies in 110 feet of water east of Erie. We wondered if it would be shrouded like the *Indiana* or it if might be as clear as the *Atlantic*. Less than ten minutes from the *Atlantic*, we were able to spot a white dive marker. As we approached, we were treated to the visible profile of the ship. We circled back over the *Dean Richmond*, taking pictures, and then headed for the airport.

Less than an hour after takeoff, we were drinking coffee in the air charter office and reviewing photographs. The mystery of why we couldn't see the *Rob Roy* or *Indiana* seemed explainable when we consulted charts and satellite images of the lake, noting bottom composition and depths. The relatively shallow, sandy bottom near those wrecks had apparently clouded the water. In the case of the deeper wrecks, *Atlantic* and *Dean Richmond*, the depth and bottom structure apparently created better clarity. In addition, the height of the two deep-water wrecks off the bottom (thirty feet or more as compared with the broken down hulls of *Rob Roy* and *Indiana*) cast underwater shadows that made their hulls stand out. The photographs were a disappointment. If we had not seen the wrecks ourselves, we would not have been convinced by the pictures.

An interesting insight occurred as I was driving home. I had just circled a huge swath of Lake Erie and visited sites where four major tragedies occurred. In less than fifteen minutes, we had traveled from the submerged *Dean Richmond* to Erie's channel entrance and landed at the airport west of the city. From the air on a clear day, the *Dean Richmond* seemed so close to shore and the channel that it was almost impossible to imagine that seasoned sailors had perished there. An early season water skier in a wet suit covered most of the distance between the *Dean Richmond* and Erie while we were taking pictures. Between the wreck and the shoreline, a pair of kayakers paddled along, blissfully unaware of the terror that had taken place at the very location more than one hundred years ago.

A few years ago, I was in Port Dover on my sailboat with a young grandson as my only crew. We awoke on the day we had planned to return to Erie to the tune of banging halyards and bending trees branches. An Erie friend who was berthed next to us stepped from his boat, held a wet finger up and pronounced the day windy. "Still going back, today?" he asked.

"We'll probably wait," I answered. "We're a bit shorthanded."

An hour later, we sat on the Port Dover Pier watching giant combers roll into the harbor while my friend hobby-horsed his way into a black, nasty-looking lake. He didn't look very happy as he waved to us. A few hundred yards from the channel, he put up a single sail and began slogging toward the tip of Long Point.

The next day, my grandson and I enjoyed a wonderful, seven-hour sail home in a steady fifteen-knot breeze. It was a glorious blue-sky day. Shortly after our arrival, we ran into my friend. He told us that he had spent fourteen hours beating his way through a twenty-five-knot southwesterly only to find himself eight miles east of Erie. Strong winds and currents had pushed him off course to the east. A pounding upwind engine ride from near the site of the *Dean Richmond* to the Erie Channel lasted another five hours and took a terrible toll on his stomach. Just before we parted that day, he mentioned that his boat was for sale.

One of the most powerful lessons of the *Dean Richmond* and many other Lake Erie shipwreck stories is the importance of patience. Was the *Dean Richmond* doomed because it left port on Friday the thirteenth or because its captain, like my sailing friend, was in a rush?

Eulogy for the Beachcomber: Goodbye Old Friend

At the request of Dave's children. I read this eulogy at his funeral service in 2007.

September 2001. Dave Stone and I are screaming across Long Point's Inner Bay in his twenty-foot aluminum boat, *Beachcomber*, fast approaching an informally marked channel through the sandbar that separates the Inner Bay from the open waters beyond. As we rush toward the shallows, Dave seems distracted. His head jerks back and forth, and his touch on the wheel is tenuous.

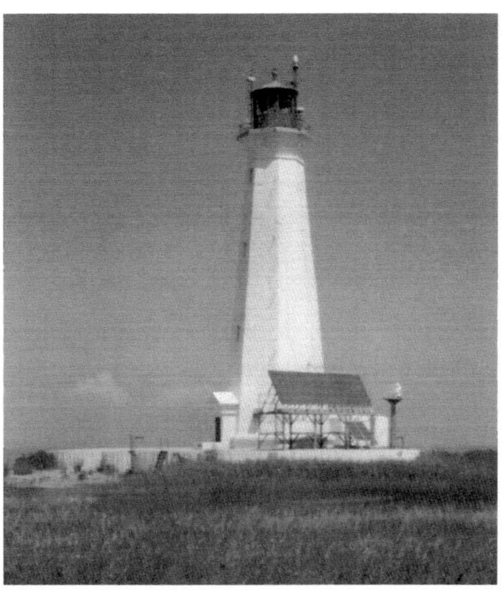

Long Point Lighthouse marked the eastern end of Dave Stone's wilderness paradise and adventureland. *Photograph by Jerry Skrypzak.*

The span of open water between Turkey Point and Pottahawk is deceptively shallow. For most of the inviting opening, depths are two feet or less, and at our speed, a grounding would be disastrous. Dave and I had made this trek countless times, but something about today is making me nervous.

I finally blurt it out: "Dave, do you see the channel opening?"

An anchored, five-gallon plastic drum is all that marks the "unofficial" channel, and we are on course to miss it by at least a half mile. Dave slows *Beachcomber* to a crawl, and for the first time in fifteen years, he steps away from the wheel. "Maybe you'd better take her through," he answers. "Eyes are watering up today."

It was one of my ritual visits to see Dave that summer, part of a pattern that we had established years earlier. I would leave Erie at 5:00 a.m. and arrive at Dave's cottage by 10:00 a.m., where I would find him pacing impatiently. Waiting for me. After coffee and a chat with his wife, Jean, Dave and I would head down the road to his boathouse, push *Beachcomber* into the cut and be away on a trek along the north side of Long Point. Through the Inner Bay to Pottahawk, a quick visit to the Millionaires' Club and then stops at the cabins along the beaches on the way to the tip of the point. We would stop to look at anything new, drag the boat onto beach locations and walk the dunes. For a magical day, we were kids with a powerboat exploring nooks and crannies and dreaming about pirates, fishermen and shipwrecks. When we encountered keepers or ministry patrols, Dave would flash his famous smile, wave his archaeological permit and break into stories. If he spotted anyone at the Anderson Cottages or the Bluffs Club, he would pull up to shore, leap from the boat and renew friendships that spanned decades.

After a day on the north side of Long Point, we would return to his cottage, get a night's sleep and awake the next morning to launch Dave's small boat from the south beach. Runs along the south side of Long Point were always fruitful. Bits of shipwrecks on deserted beaches, exposed schooner ribs and other treasures would always present themselves. It's hard to count the number of times that we stacked fish floats, winter poles and bits of shipwreck driftwood into Dave's twelve-foot runabout and dragged them back to his cottage to the chagrin of Jean Stone.

I mostly went for the stories and never tired of hearing them, even when they were repeated. For me, Dave was a magic man, a storytelling wizard, constantly regaling his willing protégé with treasures. I marveled at his energy. The 130-pound, chain-smoking man who seemed to drag himself around his cottage would become a dancer when he touched a sandy beach or dune. Nimble. Full of life. Even though the skinny relic of the 200-pound Dave Stone from earlier years had suffered a long series of health maladies and appeared to be shrinking before my eyes, when he stepped onto Long Point, he morphed into the young man that I imagined he had been at thirty. I was strong, in shape and twenty years younger, but I could barely keep up.

On this particular September day, however, Dave was moving slowly. Lost in thought and unusually quiet. Our typical four-hour tour stretched to six. He spent extra time at each stop, seeming to savor the experiences. By the time we left the tip of Long Point, it was almost dark, and Dave made a joke. "Don't know if my eyes are getting bad or its getting dark," he laughed. "Maybe you better drive."

After I took the wheel, Dave had me guide *Beachcomber* around Bluff Bar and into the Inner Bay, but when we had cleared the channel at Pottahawk, he took the wheel again. Standing with his face to the wind, he pulled the throttle hard, throwing me back against the seats. Gripping the windshield with clenched fists, we both stood bracing ourselves as we raced toward the head of the Inner Bay.

When we returned to the cottage, Jean was visibly worried. We had been gone too long, and concern for Dave showed on her face. Dave reassured her and then slipped into his study, where I could see that he was making an entry in his ship's log. Dave kept a meticulous record of every trip he had ever taken in his boats, and from my vantage point at the table, where I was helping place silverware and dishes, I could see him bent over his desk. After an unusually long time, Dave emerged with a copy of *Long Point Last Port of Call.*

"Pack this away with your stuff," he said, "but don't read my note until you get back to Erie."

Although it was difficult, I honored Dave's wish. A day later, I dragged my bag into the house and reached for the book. There on the inside cover was an inscription that heralded the first of many deaths for Dave Stone. It was to be a lesson in aging and the losses that we inevitably experience on life's journey:

> *To my good friend, Dave Frew: It's been fifteen years since our first trip to Long Point. Where does the time go? Do you remember when we almost got shipwrecked on the beaches of Long Point in the little boat? Thanks for keeping an old guy writing.*
>
> *Dave Stone*

Dave's health had been delicate for years, and after reading the inscription, I was convinced that he had just received some kind of death sentence. Suddenly, his strange behavior began to make sense. I called the next day, but there was no answer. Had he been taken away? Was he in the hospital? Had I seen him for the last time? I tried to reach his kids but failed. A day later, Dave called, chipper as ever, and made a joke. He had been diagnosed with macular degeneration and knew when we were taking *Beachcomber* out that it was to be his last trip. When his doctor had taken his driver's license the previous day, Dave, in true Stone style, asked him to hurry because he was double-parked with a school bus full of kids. By the time Dave called, he had already sold his beloved *Beachcomber* and the boathouse. There would be no more trips through the Inner Bay.

"Don't worry," he told me a week later. "This macular degeneration thing is perfect for driving my outboard along the beach. When I sit sideways and hold the motor handle, I can see straight ahead using peripheral vision," he laughed.

Dave Stone wasn't kidding. Trips along the south beaches continued as he devised ways to live on Long Point without fore and aft vision. He continued to amaze me as his vision slipped away. He purchased a three-wheeler bike so that he could get around and adorned it with accessories that he had removed from *Beachcomber*. Dave organized his tools so that he could continue to work on the cottage, and he purchased a computer screen the size of a refrigerator so that he could write. Thanks to Jean, he had transportation, and he wasn't going to let a little thing like going blind get in the way of life at Long Point.

Dave's next death came when his wife began to fail a few years later. Slowly, Jean Stone began to show signs of disorientation. For the first time since I had known them, the rock that had always anchored Dave Stone's life was beginning to crumble. Jean still went to Long Point during the summer, but she slept more. When she stopped driving, I worried. They were living on Long Point during desolate shoulder seasons, alone, without transportation and helpless. Dave's dedication to his wife during those years was inspirational. As Jean failed, there was an incredible role reversal in their marriage. Dave became the rock, caring meticulously for Jean. Frail, weak and with failing eyesight, he engineered ways to be a wonderful caretaker. When Jean finally passed away at their winter home in Ingersoll, Ontario, Dave collapsed from exhaustion and pneumonia. Most of us assumed that he would never be the same again.

Six months after Jean's death, friends convinced Dave Stone that he should return to Long Point for at least one more season. Depressed and unsure of himself, he reluctantly allowed his Ingersoll buddies to drive him to Long Point, spring-clean his cottage and deposit him at the place that he had always loved the most. They left him alone after an overnight but returned to Ingersoll wondering if he would be able to survive by himself. I visited in May and again in July, and his transformation was amazing. The depressed and lonely man I had seen in May was alive again, walking the beaches, taking his small boat out and gardening. Dave Stone had survived another death.

In early winter of 2005, I visited Dave in Ingersoll. Something was different, but I couldn't put my finger on it. After an hour of chatting, Dave proudly announced that he had quit smoking. After seventy-some years of cigarettes, he had gone "cold turkey." He was pleased with himself. I visited again in the spring, and he was a new man, full of energy and vigor. As we did chores at the cottage, he told me that he should have stopped smoking years before. He was a man possessed, intent on cleaning up the cottage for his kids before their summer visits began.

In June, I phoned to schedule another visit, and his voice was strong and enthusiastic. I began the call with a perfunctory question about how he was feeling—one that had always been answered with a cheery response, even when it was obvious that he wasn't doing well. His answer stunned me.

"Feeling great!" he responded. "Best I've felt in years. But I have cancer." Typical Dave Stone. Bad news imbedded in good. But given his cheerfulness, I presumed that he was going to tell me that it was a removable skin lesion or some other treatable malignancy. His tone grew serious, reminiscent of the days when he was taking care of Jean. It wasn't an easy, curable cancer. It was grim. Dave faced the prospects of harsh chemo and radiation therapies that might spoil the summer that could be his last on Long Point. And even with treatment, his prospects were not good.

"Why would I make things tough on my kids, have my hair and eyebrows fall out and be sick as a dog during my last year on Long Point?" he asked. "I'm eighty-three years old and probably going to die anyway," he added as we talked. Why? Because he was Dave Stone, tough guy and fighter. Ultimately, he decided to split the difference. Take a risk and begin treatment. See how it might go.

"Maybe you can get another year or two at the cottage," I suggested.

His kids encouraged him, and he went for it, putting up a gallant fight. Gave it everything that a skinny eighty-three-year-old had to offer. As the treatments consumed him, Dave Stone seemed satisfied with a life well lived. The jokes continued to the end. When he passed, no one was surprised to learn that Dave had asked to have his ashes spread on Long Point.

Dave Stone changed my life. I will always remember our first meetings. Tracking down the "Beachcomber of Long Point," author, storyteller and creator of the famous shipwreck map. I can still see him speaking to over-capacity crowds at Gannon University, charming them with stories of ships and shipwrecks. But mostly I will remember Dave Stone the dancer, bounding gracefully from his boat, leading me up and over Long Point's sand ridges. Telling stories.

For me, Dave Stone will always be Long Point, the mysterious peninsula that I see from Erie on clear fall days. He will be there in spirit and body.

Dave Stone, 1923–2007

EPILOGUE

THE SEARCH GOES ON

There will never be another shipwreck era like that of the nineteenth century. Modern technology, including incredibly accurate weather forecasting, will prevent the losses that Lake Erie witnessed during the one-hundred-year period between the end of the War of 1812 and the early 1900s. The evolution of modern one-thousand-foot bulk ships that began in the 1970s has also contributed. Each of the new jumbo ships has replaced a dozen smaller vessels, most of which were far less structurally sound than the new breed of super ships.

The virtual end of shipwrecks does not, however, spell the end of adventure. Thanks to a new generation of wreck hunters like the Wachters, who are more interested in the stories of Lake Erie wrecks than souvenir gathering, the search will continue. The Wachters have been generous, providing underwater photographs and GPS locations, thus inspiring others to join the hunt. Their book series lists wrecks, summarizes stories and describes the wrecks as dive sites. As more are located, we will all benefit from the stories that will emerge.

Of the thousands of recorded Lake Erie wrecks, the Watchers currently list 103 diveable and recognizable wrecks, which leaves many more to be uncovered. How many is unclear, but that is a continuing part of the mystery.

As this book was going to press, Eric Guerrin, who runs Lakeshore Towing and Salvage, provided a sketch of the last Lake Erie shipwreck, the *Carol Sue II*. The *Carol Sue* was a sixty-three-foot wooden work tug launched during 1926 in the Chesapeake Bay. New owners purchased and refitted

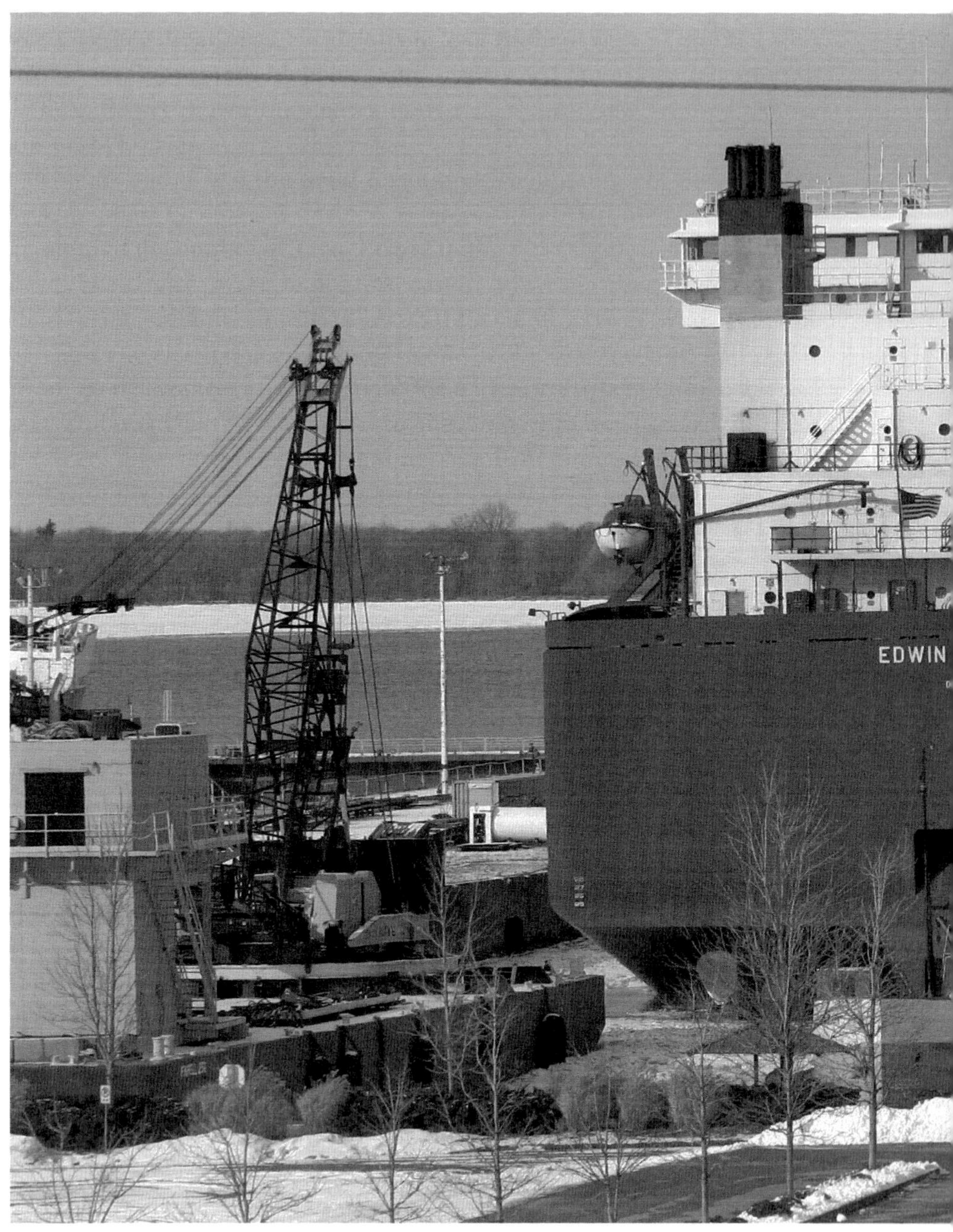

Thousand-foot bulk ships like the *Edwin Gott*, shown here at Erie, have significantly reduced shipping traffic on the Great Lakes. *Photograph by Jerry Skrypzak.*

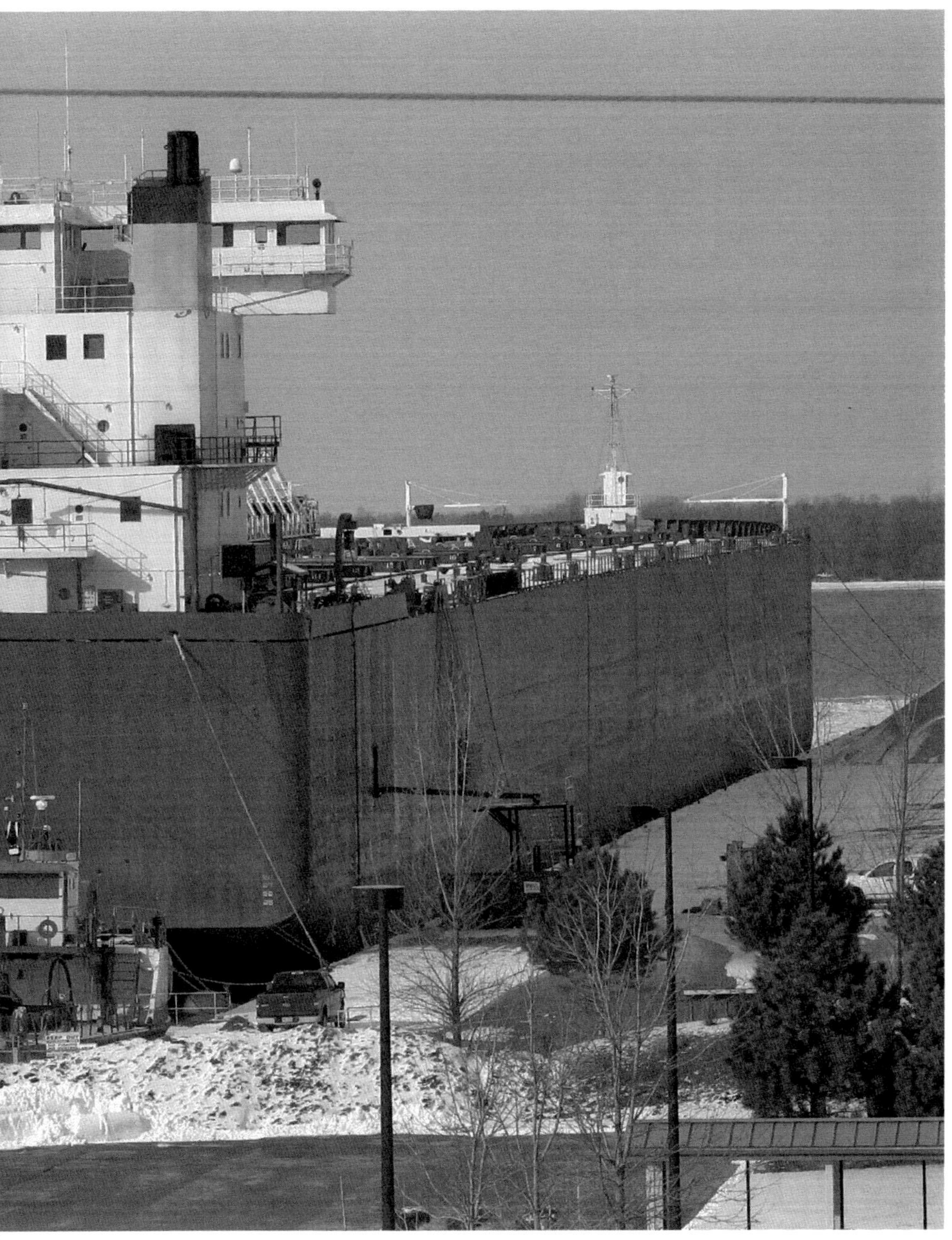

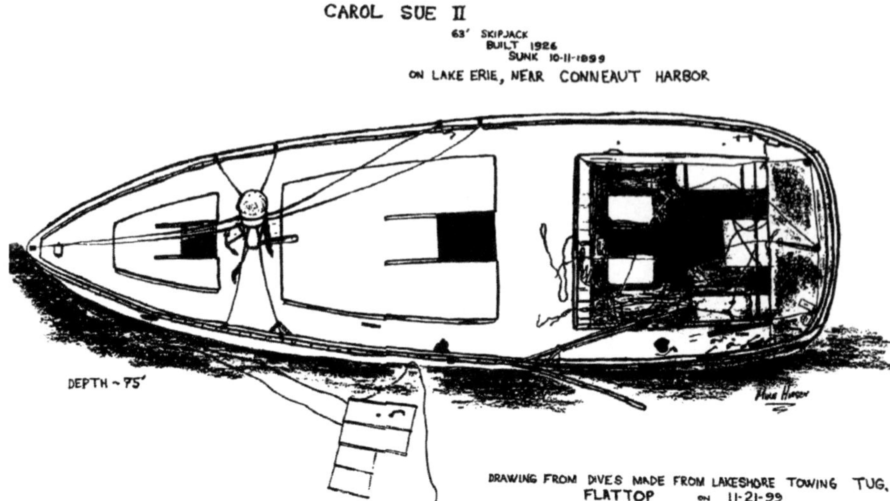

Sketch of the sunken *Carol Sue II*. *Courtesy of Eric Guerrein and Lakeshore Towing.*

it as a charter boat and brought it to Sandusky, Ohio, but their business was faltering because of the short northern season. On October 11, 1999, as the boat was being moved from Ohio to Norfolk, Virginia, the delivery crew suddenly found that it was taking on water. In less than five minutes, the *Carol Sue II* sank just east of the Ohio/Pennsylvania state line. The crew members took to the water, where they held on to the wheelhouse, which floated free of the sinking ship. They were ultimately rescued by the Erie Coast Guard.

The wreck of the *Carol Sue II* fifteen years ago may provide an indication of the expected frequency of new Lake Erie shipwrecks. Based on that timing, we might see eight or nine during the next century as opposed to the thousands that occurred between 1812 and the early 1900s.

The one important Lake Erie wreck that currently eludes divers but is almost certainly lying on the floor of Lake Erie waiting to be discovered is the *Marquette & Bessemer No. 2*, which disappeared more than one hundred years ago. Many, including myself, have speculated on its likely location, but as of the time of publication of this book, the *Marquette & Bessemer No. 2* remains the "holy grail" of Lake Erie shipwrecks—or perhaps Great Lakes shipwrecks, if the location of LaSalle's *Griffon* has actually been found, as has been asserted by divers from Lake Michigan. And when the Lake Erie car-ferry is found, the location, as is the case with each newly discovered wreck location, will help those who have wondered about the events of its sinking to piece together the strange events of the loss. In the days and months after the car-ferry disappeared, lifeboats were discovered at various locations, a debris field floated down the center of the lake and crew washed ashore months and years later.

Some years ago, I had the good fortune to accompany Dr. Steve Blasco of the Canadian Geological Service as he and Rob Cromwell, from Port Dover, scoured the bottom of Lake Erie with the most sophisticated scanners available. His devices were many times more powerful than any scanners that had been used previously. Blasco's official objectives were partially geological, as he charted deep ice scours on the floor of the lake, and partly technical, as he worked to engineer a "best" track for lake-floor cables to connect Ontario Power Generation to the United States power grid. But as we talked, it became apparent that he, like Rob Cromwell, had become infected with the mystery of the *Marquette & Bessemer.*

"How could a three-hundred-foot steel ship carrying thirty railroad cars simply disappear in Lake Erie and remain lost for so long?" he asked one afternoon. "Especially given the frenetic search that has continued for more than one hundred years."

Steve Blasco has not given up, and perhaps it will be a scientist like him who will find it someday. That was, after all, how Dr. Robert Ballard found the *Titanic*—as a serendipitous artifact of his search for the missing nuclear submarine *Thresher* in the North Atlantic. A few years after Dave Stone spoke at my university, I invited Bob Ballard to talk about his search for the *Titanic*, and over breakfast the next morning, I shared my research file on the *Marquette & Bessemer*. A few days after he left Erie, he called to tell me that he could not believe that the old car-ferry could not be found and promised to come back someday.

While we wait, both dive and location technology becomes increasingly sophisticated. Lake Erie will continue to reveal its mysteries, and I, for one, can't wait!

BIBLIOGRAPHY

Barrett, Harry B. *Legend and Lore of Long Point.* Don Mills, ON: Burns and MacEachern, 1977.

Berman, B. *Encyclopedia of American Shipwrecks.* Boston: Mariners Press, 1973.

Boyer, D. *Great Stories of the Great Lakes.* New York: Mead, 1966.

Chapelle, H. *History of American Sailing Ships.* New York: Bonanza Books, 1935.

Erie Dispatch News. Select Archival Materials, Erie Public Library.

Erie Times News. Select Archival Materials, Erie Public Library.

Frew, David. *Kiss of the Devil Wind: Sinking of the Gerkin.* Erie, PA: Erie County Historical Society, 2000.

———. *Long Gone: The Mystery of the* Marquette & Bessemer No. 2. Erie, PA: Erie County Historical Society, 2002.

———. *Perry's Lake Erie Fleet: After the Glory.* Charleston, SC: The History Press, 2012.

Greenwood, John. *Greenwood Guide to Great Lakes Shipping.* Cleveland, OH: Freshwater Press, 1987.

Hancock, P. *Shipwrecks of the Great Lakes.* Thunder Bay, ON: Thunder Bay Press, 2001.

Journal of Erie Studies. Select Archival Materials. Erie, PA: Erie County Historical Society. Available at the ECHS Library.

Lapinski, Patrick. *Great Lakes Shipping.* Hudson, WI: Iconographics, 2011.

Lloyd's of London. *Market Resources Reports*. London, 1900–36. Available by order from Lloyd's.

Lloyd's Steamboat Directory and Disasters. Cincinnati, OH: Lloyd and Company, 1856.

Malcomson, Robert. *Warships of the Great Lakes.* London: Chathom Publishing, 2001.

Port Dover Maple Leaf. Select Archival Materials. Port Dover, Ontario.

The Robert McDonald Collection. Erie County Historical Society, Erie, Pennsylvania.

Roosevelt, Theodore. *The Naval War of 1812.* New York: Putnam, 1882.

Rybka, Walter. *The Lake Erie Campaign of 1813: We Will Fight Them This Day.* Charleston, SC: The History Press 2012.

Stone, Dave. *Long Point: Last Port of Call.* Erin, ON: Boston Mills Press, 1988.

Stone, Dave, and David Frew. *The Lake Erie Quadrangle: Waters of Repose.* Erie, PA: Erie County Historical Society, 1993.

Stonehouse, F. *Steel on the Bottom.* Avery, MI: Avery Studios, 2006.

Swayze, David. *Shipwreck.* Boyne City, MI: Harbor House, 1992.

United States Government Printing Office. *Merchant Vessels of the United States.* Washington, D.C.: self-published, 2012.

Wachter, Georgann, and Michael Wachter. *Erie Wrecks East.* Avon Lake, OH: Impact Press, 2003.

INDEX

P

R

S

T

U

V

W

ABOUT THE AUTHOR

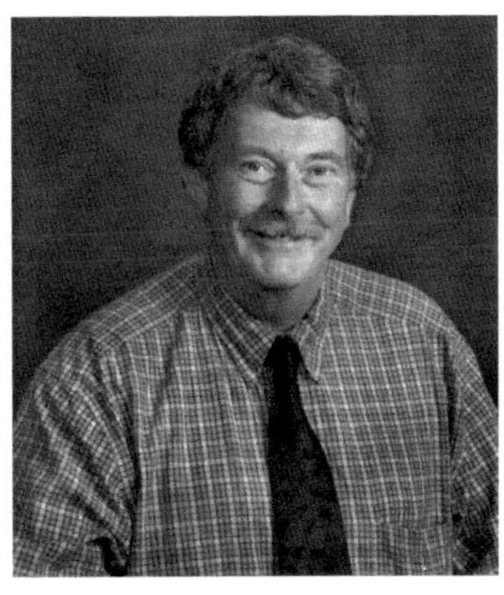

Dr. David Frew is a visiting professor at Mercyhurst University in Erie, Pennsylvania. He is also an emeritus professor at Gannon University, where he served on the faculty and held a variety of administrative positions during a thirty-three-year career; emeritus director of the Erie County Historical Society; and president of his own management consulting business. He has authored or coauthored thirty-seven books and more than one hundred articles, cases and papers. His work has appeared in publications ranging from peer-reviewed journals such as the *Journal of Applied Psychology* to popular magazines including *Sail* magazine and *Cruising World*. His books on Lake Erie ships, shipping and shipwrecks represent a narrative history of the industries that formed the backbone of the Great Lakes maritime economy. He is married and has three grown children, eight grandchildren and one great-grandson. He is an avid racing and cruising sailor and a competitive club-level, four-wall handball player.